RELIGION
A Secular Theory

RELIGION
A Secular Theory

Andrew M. Greeley

THE FREE PRESS
A Division of Macmillan Publishing Co., Inc.
New York

Collier Macmillan Publishers
London

The Free Press
A Division of Macmillan Publishing Co., Inc.
866 Third Avenue, New York, N.Y. 10022

Collier Macmillan Canada, Ltd.

Library of Congress Catalog Number: 81-67329

Printed in the United States of America

printing number

1 2 3 4 5 6 7 8 9 10

Library of Congress Cataloging in Publication Data

Greeley, Andrew M.
   Religion, a secular theory.

   Bibliography: p.
   Includes index.
   1. Religion and sociology. I. Title.
BL60.G72   306'.6   81-67329
ISBN 0-02-912870-6   AACR2
ISBN 0-02-912880-3 (pbk.)

Contents

Acknowledgments

I am especially grateful to John Shea, David Tracy, Bruno Manno, William McCready, and my sibling, Mary Durkin, for their insights and ideas, from which I have stolen liberally—I hope always with proper acknowledgments. I also wish to thank my students in Sociology 322 at the University of Arizona in the spring of 1980 for their enormous contribution to the development of this book, which was used for the first time as a textbook in that course. The names of the students, as I promised them, are printed below:

Roza Marie Abbasi
Laree A. Adkins
Robin Ann Agers
Joseph Francis Allen
Carey Anne Angland
Marguerite Schaaf Bantlin
Theora Ruth Litt Barringer
Terri Ann Bauer
Margaret Ann Bedrosian
Doug Scott Bradley
Peter Edward Brixie
Glen Robert Broemer
Norman Lyall Bruneau
Charles Edward Byers
Theresa Jane Byrne
Henri Louis Capdeville
Rita Mary Caracciolo
Charlotte Lowe Cheatham

Andrea Lee Cohen
John David Curry
Kristin Gray Davis
Catherine Mary Dewar
Constance Lea Dresdow
Hustin Joseph Dyer Jr.
Charles Maurice Eavenson
Susan Engelman
Linda Therese Eger
Jay Scott Flagg
Suzanne Constance Forbes
Louise M. Moore Forland
Shari Ann Funess
Catherine Therese Gaytan
Sally M. Milne Gething
Michael George Glaser
Andrew N. Greifer
Sandra Lee Gwin

Acknowledgments

Peter John Halvin
Robert Lynn Harper
Raquel Linfird Hoffman
Jedediah Dunning Holdorph II
Sheila Muriel Hook
James Robert Immer
Mary Margaret Kelley
David S. Lane
Howard J. Levinson
Stephen John Lovett
Philip Lum
Suzanne Marie MacLean
Margaret Mary Maher
Lyetta Suzanne Mathews
Carol Sue McGuire
Bruce Allen Munroe
Constance T. Needham
Krista Ann Perry Neis
Sheryl Beth Newman
Liza Anne Nussbaum
Mary Ann O'Neil
William David Ortega
Sister Marie Adele O'Sullivan
Tina Marie Pajkos
Kathryn M. Peck
Ray Vaughan Pyle II

Charles Wayne Ratliff
Jonathan William Reich
Brian Joseph Ricci
Robert Brian Roden
Barbara Lloyd Rogers
Cynthia Margaret Rummel
Colin John Samson
Kathleen Susan Schweppe
Elizabeth Anna Shestko
Leslie Anne Shultz
Karlene Mary Smith
Walter Thomas Stash III
Craig Alan Steveley
Gregoy Alan Stewart
Kayellen Stott
Margaret Jean Sturm
Doug Leonard Wagley
Gale Renee Walden
Thomas Arvin Warren
Valerie Elizabeth Weiler
Elizabeth Weiss
Therese Marie Welchert
John Lawrnece Westenhaver
Loti Maureen Shea Wilcox
Linda Ellen Wilson

I also wish to thank Mary Kotecki and Ruth Schwartz for help in preparation of the manuscript.

RELIGION
A Secular Theory

Chapter One
Introduction

It is the purpose of this book to present a social science theory of religion. A number of preliminary comments are in order:

1. My theory is a "secular" theory. By that I do not mean a theory of "secularization"—a theory which asserts that religion is less important than it used to be at some usually unspecified times in the past. Nor does my theory oppose the "secular" to the "sacred," as though the profane and the holy are two sharply delineated spheres. On the contrary I believe that while the secular and the sacred are somewhat distinct, the boundaries between the two are amorphous and permeable. The secular intrudes into the sacred, and the sacred into the secular every day.

Rather, I oppose the secular to the ecclesiastical. Religion, I will argue in my theory, is part of daily life anterior to and more important than the trappings which ecclesiastical institutions add to it. You do not find religion in church, or if you do, ordinarily what you find is religious only secondarily and derivatively. The rise of formal religious institutions in complex societies, I will argue in this book, is inevitable and necessary. Furthermore, churches play an important role in shaping the context in which an individual person's or a family's religious "story" emerges, because the church is one of those institutions which passes on (sometimes in very abstract and distorted fashions) the religious stories that an individual person or a family or a small community absorbs and makes the "story" of his or her or their lives. The family

1

is a more important institution of religious socialization than the church. But, the church is still important.

The church is more a result of religion than its cause. The scholar studying religion and the ordinary person trying to understand religion ought not to begin by looking at churches or denominations. They ought, rather, to begin by looking at the experiences of daily life in which religion takes its roots and from which it draws its enormous power.

2. My theory will be a "model" of religion. Indeed, it will be a model about religious models. I intend to suggest that religious "stories" are models for interpreting and shaping human life. By model I mean an oversimplified and schematized design or template or pattern which provides a useful perspective for understanding certain phenomena. The wave theory of electromagnetism, Marx's theory of class conflict, Freud's tripartite personality of Id, Ego, and Superego are all models. As Ian Barbour has pointed out in his *Myths, Models and Religion,* "A model purports to be neither a total and absolute description of reality, nor merely a pattern which exists only in the mind of the model builder and need bear no relationship to the real other than that of the useful, intellectual tool."

A model is a provisional but incomplete description of reality which is subject both to modification and possible rejection as we learn more about the real; it is also subject to the competition of complimentary models. Thus, physicists no longer feel the need to choose between the wave and the quantum theories of electromagnetism, but find that both are useful approaches to the description of electromagnetic phenomena. Many historians and sociologists are willing to use Marx's class conflict model as a useful perspective from which to examine the social order, and a perspective which tells us many important things about that order, but they supplement class conflict with other perspectives which can account for elements and dimensions of human behavior that cannot be subsumed under a class conflict perspective.

2

Similarly, social scientist Paul Peterson has recently described school board politics in the city of Chicago using four different models. Peterson contends, persuasively it seems to me, that each different perspective reveals something about the nature of such politics that would be missed if one excluded that perspective from one's consideration. Are all the perspectives true? Peterson seems to imply that each of them helps us to see part of the truth. Are some more true than others? Unless I misunderstand Peterson, he seems to be implying that it really doesn't matter, so long as they are all useful, and provisionally and partly (in the sense of revealing part) true.

Hence, I am making no claim that my model of religion is the only one that is appropriate, not even the only appropriate social science model. It is, rather, a provisional and incomplete description of religious reality, open to being complemented and supplemented by other social science models as well as models from other viewpoints and disciplines. As a sociologist, I use the model of religion that I will present in this volume. As a human being, I use other models which do not necessarily contradict the one I shall describe, but complement and, perhaps, critique it. Therefore, it is not a valid reaction to this book to say that there are other and more useful and, perhaps, even more true ways of viewing religion. I cheerfully concede that point to begin with. I merely assert that the theory presented in this volume is a useful and provisionally and partly (again in describing part of the matter) true schematization of religious reality.

3. My theory will deal with "stories of God" (to use the title of a book by John Shea). I will contend that the primordial religious imagery in the human creative preconscious exists in the form of stories. To say that religion is a story, however, is not to say that it is a fairy tale or a fable or a legend which bears no relation to the real world. The religious story purports to be true in the sense that it claims to provide a description and, indeed, a uniquely valid descrip-

tion of the Way Things Really Are. In colorful and dramatic language—a language different from that of, let us say, the physical or social sciences—religious stories purport to interpret the meaning of the cosmos, the meaning of personal existence and the appropriate patterns for human behavior (as Bruno Bettelheim has recently demonstrated, fairy stories do, indeed, purport to do the same thing and are, if not quite the same thing as religious stories, first cousins to them).

When the ancient said that the cosmos was the result of a battle between a demi-God and the dragon of chaos, he was asserting in vivid language his conviction that Whoever or Whatever was responsible for Things assumed this responsibility by imposing Order on Chaos—usually a highly tentative and tenuous order. Not being as (perhaps obsessively) compulsive about his language or about his distinctions as the modern, the ancient may not have self-consciously distinguished as does the modern between the language and the images of religion and the language and images of other activities. Yet, he used a different approach in his religious stories than he did in repeating instructions on how to build a canoe—though at times even canoe construction might be blended into religious story and ritual.

Although religion is primordial story, it is not fiction (there may be some truth in the opposite assertion that good fiction and, often, not so good fiction is latently religious in that it provides implicitly, and often not so implicitly, provisional explanations of the meaning of the cosmos). It does matter to the teller of a religious story that it is true in the sense that it portrays the Real. He does not, however, purport to present the Real the way the writer of an historical monograph would, or the way a journalist would in writing for the *New York Times* or the CBS Evening News.

In the case of the historical religions—Christianity, Judaism, and Islam—the matter is more complex. For these religions claim their stories are not only true in the sense of being accurate, if poetic descriptions, of the cosmos and of

4

personal existence, but also true in the sense that such stories correspond to and are related with events that actually and factually occurred in historical times. The chosen people did, indeed, covenant with Jaweh in the Sinai; Jesus did, indeed, die and rise again; Mohammed did make his pilgrimage from Mecca to Medinah. However, even in an historical religion the claim to factuality, while essential, is not paramount. The religious stories of Christianity, Judaism, and Islam are fundamentally stories of the meaning of reality in addition to being (frequently poetic and highly theologised) descriptions of factual events which confirm the validity of the stories as Models for the Real. The Christian story of the resurrection of Jesus is more important for its implication about the purposes and the destiny of life than it is as a description of an historical event.

Even in the historical religions there is a willingness to admit that the stories need to be interpreted, both because the language in which they are presented is different from the language of our own times and very different from the historical language of our own times, and, also, because we live in an era of what Paul Ricoeur calls the transition between the first and the second "naivete," a time when it is necessary to take apart and subject to precise, critical scrutiny the components of a religious story before we can put those components back together again and use them as models for life.

Therefore, it will be clear to the reader that when I refer to religious stories I am not questioning their accuracy or their factuality. Religious stories claim to be true. Indeed, as Clifford Geertz has put it, they claim to be "uniquely" true. Whether they are, in fact, true or not is a matter which goes beyond social science and, indeed, even beyond theology, and depends finally on the personal decision of the individual. The evidence available to a social scientist can enable him to say that religious stories claim to be uniquely accurate and factual (if highly colored) descriptions of the Way Things Really Are. Sociological data, however, and sociological theory do not permit any judgments pro or con about the validity of that claim. If many, perhaps most, social scientists do not accept personally the claim to validity of religious stories then absence of faith has nothing to do with their social science and cannot be confirmed by it (nor refuted by it either); since this book is an exercise in social science and not in religious story-telling and reflection (exercises in which I engage elsewhere), I will make no attempt in it to argue for the validity or the non-validity of religious stories as explanations of Existence.

My refusal to enter into the question of validity of religious stories may offend the religious believer (particularly of the fundamentalist or evangelical variety) who insists on commitments explicitly made at any and all times. It may also offend some social science scholars who seem convinced that scholarly objectivity about religion requires faintly contemptuous skepticism and/or agnosticism. Some such scholars would even go so far as to contend that one cannot be a committed believer and be objective about religion (at least as moderately objective as is required to write a book of social science theory). They fail to explain why one can be a convinced unbeliever and be professionally objective.

For the record, so that no one might accuse me of hiding the ground on which I stand, I will assert that while the Good News in my own personal stories of religion may seem too good to be true, it is nonetheless true. It suffers as a model of Ultimate Reality only one defect: the Good News is even better than we think it is. Having thus stated my own personal religious perspective and having acknowledged that it creates for me as a social theorist of religion both problems and possibilities that the unbelieving scholar would not have (though he has both problems and possibilities that I do not have), I will prescind for the rest of this book from matters of personal faith.

4. While my theory of religion is sociological, it will

search out sources and perspectives which most sociological theories of religion—to their detriment, I believe—do not use. Having discussed Marx, Weber and Durkheim, and, perhaps, Comte and Simmel, most contemporary sociologists of religion in the United States are willing to go on to Talcott Parsons and, perhaps, Robert Bellah and Charles Y. Glock, ignoring mostly out of ignorance, I fear, the religious insights of anthropology, psychology, literary criticism, philosophy, and theology. The result, it must be admitted, is work which looks to the scholars of other disciplines to be incredibly naive. My own viewpoint as a sociologist is, I suppose, ultimately traceable to Max Weber, as filtered through Talcott Parsons and Clifford Geertz. As will be clear in this volume, I find Durkheim useful in some respects (which is more than I can say for either Bellah or Glock). But I see no reason why sociologists should deprive themselves of the insights and intellectual tools provided by such non-sociological scholars as Clifford Geertz, Sten Stenson, Ian Barbour, or Ricoeur, Mircea Eliade, David Tracy, and John Shea. There is nothing in the work of these scholars, for example, which in any way conflicts with sound sociological theory, and much complements it, illumines it, and enriches it. Failure of most sociological scholars to make use of the work of such men is parochialism at its worst.

5. My theory is, however, still basically constructed from the point of view of a sociologist. My initial chapters may seem more social-psychological and cultural because they deal with the religious experiences of the individual personality. I insist that even these experiences are both shaped by the cultural and structural background of a person and in turn shape both the perspectives from which he deals with his life and the established relationship patterns to which he commits himself.

In subsequent chapters I will become more sociological as I deal with the development of "common religious stories" which describe the religious experiences and the resonating and articulating stories of human communities, including both families and larger groups. It is rhetorically more productive first to describe the religious experience and the religious story as an individual event. But such events are influenced and to some considerable extent shaped by social and cultural factors and, also, represent in miniature large collective social and historical processes.

6. My theory will be empirical. Most of my propositions are based on empirical evidence already collected and will be subjected to testing by further evidence collection. Such an assertion cannot be made about most sociological theories of religion. It is frequently said, for example, by Robert Bellah and by others that the flowering of religious cults which occurred during the 1970s was the result of post-Vietnam, post-Watergate disillusionment among the liberal and radical activists of the 1960s. Such a global proposition is not really subject to falsification. When you hear it at a cocktail party, for example, how can you find evidence to refute it? Indeed, how could you go about designing a data collection process to refute it? The proposition would, perhaps, be tested if sufficient time and money were available, but it would have to be specified more precisely than it is. It is hardly the intention of those who propound it to submit it to such examination.

If an assertion does not admit of falsification, if there is no imaginable way that you can disprove it, then neither does it admit of verification, and there is no imaginable way you can prove it. It may be useful cocktail party conversation, but it is not scholarship or science. Many of the currently practicing sociologists of religion such as Peter Berger are serenely uninterested in the possibility of falsification of their propositions and utterly unencumbered and undisturbed by empirical evidence. I'm sorry, but I do not consider that to be either scholarship or science. My demand for verifiable and falsifiable propositions is not the result of the eagerness of the fact collector or the data grubber for propositions he can test.

Social theory is no more than unsure pontification unless it admits of falsification because in the absence of the possibility of falsification you cannot have verification and you cannot have truth—even provisional and partial truth.

7. My theory, I think, is consistent. There are no logical flaws or contradictions in it, or if there are any such, they have slipped in despite my efforts to exclude them. However, it is not coherent in the sense that the parts hang together in such a way that falsification or verification of one component of the theory either confirms or jeopardizes the whole theory. Social reality is too complicated to admit of such coherent theories. I prefer a more flexible "building block" approach in which some of the blocks may have to be abandoned or replaced or reshaped without the destruction of the whole edifice.

8. Similarly, I will be seen to have violated the social science demand for parsimony in my theorizing. Quite properly, social science scholars want theories that are as brief and elegant as possible. Unfortunately, that often seems to mean theories which are limited to a handful of propositions. My ninety-nine theses may seem like a very large handful. In my own defense, however, I contend that parsimony is not the only virtue in social theory and that it ought to yield to the higher norm of adequacy. Parsimony, I take it, should mean no more propositions than are necessary to adequately deal with the phenomenon. If that means ninety-six propositions, then so be it.

9. I make no assumptions in the beginning of this exercise about a proper definition of religion. There exists a bitter and useless controversy in the sociology of religion about what religion is, and whether one needs an explicit "transcendental," "superempirical" Referant for a belief system to be religious. One school of thought insists that if there is no such Referant, then a belief system is not religious, while another school of thought contends that any belief system that pur-

ports to provide ultimate meaning for human life must be considered religious whether a "superempirical" or "transcendental" Referant is presumed or not. The argument is much ado about nothing; when such ideologies as Marxism or feminism or psychoanalysis become basic belief systems for individuals, they take on a sacred and transcendental quality which makes them indistinguishable from religion. Furthermore, any definition which excludes from consideration phenomena which seem clearly to be religious is not a very useful intellectual tool. However, I do not think the definitional question ought to be answered at the beginning of an investigation. One should first find out what phenomena that are clearly religious are like, then form a definition rather than the other way around. Precise definitions, in other words, ought to be the result of an investigation and not the beginning of it. How, then, do I know what I am studying if I do not have a precise definition? I am studying those things which ordinary people commonly consider to be religious. That is not only enough to start with, it is all one can start with.

10. My theory is not evolutionary. While I am prepared to concede that there have been changes in religious behavior since the thirteenth, sixteenth, nineteenth, and even the early twentieth centuries, I do not find an evolutionary approach to such changes to be particularly fruitful, and surely not the evolutionary approach of a secularization theory which thinks that religion somehow is becoming "less important." I have dealt with this issue elsewhere (in *Unsecular Man: The Persistence of Religion*). It is sufficient to say that I will pay little attention in this volume to the secularization theory or any similar evolutionary approach. Doubtless, they may have some useful contributions to make (though, in my judgment, not very useful), but I am concerned in this work with another perspective.

11. As will be seen shortly, I have placed primordial

religious phenomena in the preconscious or the creative imagination, or the poetic dimension of the personality (or in the right hemisphere of the brain, if one wishes). I am not suggesting that religion is nonrational or irrational or superrational. I am, rather, contending that religion begins prerationally. I am not arguing against subsequent application of the rational processes to religious experiences, symbols, and stories. Quite the contrary, reasoning about religion is inevitable and necessary. However, religion does not start in the discursive intellect. If one wishes to understand religion, one must look elsewhere.

12. In this volume I will not attempt to deal with the newly fashionable "genetic" approach to religion, which contends that some of our religious propensities and some of our religious "stories" are coded in our genes. Carl Sagan has argued, for example, that the paradise myth may be a holdover in our limbus (the more primitive part of our brain) of early conflicts between the newly emergent mammals and the reptiles who had dominated the earth before the coming of the mammals. Such a suggestion is ludicrous, first of all because Professor Sagan displays no knowledge other than the most fundamentalistic interpretation of what the serpent myth means in ancient religion, and secondly, because his argument is nonscientific: it can neither be refuted nor confirmed. It is a hunch, a guess, an insight, not a scientific proposition, not unless and until Dr. Sagan can identify that part of our gene pool in which the serpent myth is encoded.

I would be inclined to take more seriously Lionel Tiger's suggestion (to which I will return in the next chapter) that we may be genetically predisposed to hopefulness. Hopefulness even in hopeless situations, indeed, especially in the most hopeless situation of the moment of death, seems to be a universal human phenomenon. I would not be surprised that a species which has acquired the capacity to reflect on its own mortality would selectively produce offspring who had some genetic predisposition to hope. Otherwise, despair might have wiped out the species long ago. But, while Professor Tiger's position is not unreasonable, neither is it confirmed nor in the present state of our knowledge confirmable. Again, one must know which gene (or gene combination) it is that predisposes us to hope.

My starting point in the next chapter will be the fact that hopefulness seems to be a given in the human condition. I will bracket the issue of whether it is genetically or culturally programed into us. However, I must note that the reductionist tendency in the genetic explanation of religion is pernicious to scholarly investigation. To have linked religion with something that our genes produced in the limbus is not to explain it, much less to explain it away (as Sagan and occasionally Tiger seem to think). Both the social science issue of the role of religion in human life and the faith issue of whether religious stories are valid or not remain to be answered. Professor Tiger seems to be convinced at least most of the time that our hope is an illusion just as Bruno Bettelheim seems convinced that the fairy tales are illusion, functional and useful illusions, perhaps, but still illusions. They are entitled to their opinions surely, but it ought to be made clear that neither Tiger's ingenious anthropology nor Bettleheim's brilliant psychoanalysis prove that their opinion is right (any more than my sociology—whatever its merits—proves that they are wrong). Both the fairy stories and the propensity to hope merely establish that there is a powerful tendency to hope in human nature, perhaps an uneradicable tendency. Whether the hope is revelation or deception, sacrament or wish-fulfillment is an issue which transcends scholarship, though it is the religious question *par excellence.* Bettelheim and Tiger seem to think we live in a cruel and arbitrary universe which capriciously tricks us into hope when there are no grounds for it. Quite possibly they are correct, but their conclusions follow from acts of faith on their own part, not from their scholarly and scientific premises. It is imperative that anyone thinking seriously about religion keep this fact firmly in mind: the conclusion that hope is a biological or psychological trick is just as much an act of faith as is the conclusion that it is revelation and sacrament.

13. Finally, I do not intend to burden myself or the reader with the pompous and tedious *apparat*—the scholarly footnote—as though a work becomes more careful, more scholarly, or more objective if one multiplies the number of references to publishers, publication dates, and the home offices of publishing companies. In an appendix I will provide bibliographic references for each chapter, noting the principal sources for my propositions.

Similarly, I do not intend this volume to be a monograph in mathematical models about religion. Hence, I will omit the tables and path diagrams, referring the reader normally to already published volumes which substantiate any propositions I make in this book.

I regret burdening the reader with this long preliminary statement. But religion, like sex, is a subject that easily generates misunderstanding and controversy. It is essential at the beginning of any serious discussion of religion that one be very precise about what one is attempting to do. A critic may wish that a writer had other intentions. If he is a book reviewer, he may lament the fact that the writer has not written the book that he himself intends to write someday. One must, nevertheless, concede to a writer the privilege of choosing his own perspective and delineating his own approach and his own boundaries. It is an ambitious enough goal, I think, to try to elaborate a sociological theory of religion without attempting simultaneously a lot of other tasks. My scope in this book is wide enough. It is necessary at the beginning to indicate what the outer boundaries of that scope are.

Chapter Two
Hope and Grace

2.1 *In the human personality there exists a propensity to hope.*

The wording of my first proposition is deliberately cautious. I make no claims that hope is uneradicable, or that hope is everywhere and always stronger than despair. Some authors would go further. The theologian Schubert Ogden says that hope is "unforfitable." The psychoanalyst Sigmund Freud says that the unconscious believes it is immortal. The anthropologist Lionel Tiger contends that we are genetically programed to hope. All of these distinguished observers of the human condition may be right, but for the purposes of my theory it is not necessary to go that far. I propose that religion is rooted in hope. Where there is hope, I suggest, there will be religion of one sort or another. Since it is not necessary for me to claim that everyone has a religious "instinct," much less a genetic religious predetermination, I do not need to go beyond the mild and easily verifiable observation that most of us tend to hope most of the time.

The death research of Dr. Elisabeth Kübler-Ross, for example, noted that a strong and growing hope was the final phase in the human personality's acclamation to the inevitability of death. Later research on resuscitation suggests that in the moment of dying and even in the moments after death hope grows stronger yet. Other scholars who have investigated near misses with sudden death report that those who go through these experiences describe them as though they were ecstatic experiences of hopefulness.

G.K. Chesterton summarized the experience that the various investigators seem to be describing.

> But in those few moments, while my cab was tearing toward the traffic of the Strand, . . . I really did have, in that short and shrieking period, a rapid succession of a number of fundamental points of view. I had, so to speak, about five religions in almost as many seconds. My first religion was pure Paganism, which among sincere men is more shortly described as extreme fear. Then there succeeded a state of mind which is quite real, but for which no proper name has ever been found. The ancients called it Stoicism, and I think it must be what some German lunatics mean (if they mean anything) when they talk about Pessimism. It was an empty and open acceptance of the thing that happens—as if one had got beyond the value of it. And then, curiously enough, came a very strong contrary feeling—that things mattered very much indeed, and yet that they were something more than tragic. It was a feeling, not that life was unimportant, but that life was much too important ever to be anything but life. I hope that this was Christianity. At any rate, it occurred at the moment when we went crash into the omnibus. ["The Accident," *Selected Essays of G.K. Chesterton.* London: Collins, 1936, p. 68]

None of the death research is based on scientific probability samples. Unfortunately, funding agencies are not yet ready to break with their secularist ideologies and take seriously such investigations. Yet, while the work has been resoundingly criticized by many other scholars, no one has denied the widespread prevalence of hopefulness. The argument has been, rather, against the conclusions that these investigators draw from their reporting on the experiences of hope. Neither have the critics of Lionel Tiger disputed his

16

contention that hope is practically universal in the human condition. They have, rather, disputed his argument that hopefulness is genetically programed into our biology.

My colleague William McCready, working with national sample data, has demonstrated that when respondents are presented with vignettes depicting life's tragedies—long illness, fatal illness, the birth of a handicapped child—four-fifths of the American population respond with optimistic or hopeful reactions (the nature of the distinction between hope and optimism will be discussed later). Angry, pessimistic, and resigned response patterns to questions about the meaning of tragedy dominate less than a fifth of McCready's respondents. Hope may not be genetically programed as Tiger suggests or psychologically inevitable as a psychoanalysist may argue. It may not even be statistically universal. It is, nonetheless, widespread—and as McCready indicates, the optimistic and hopeful portions of the population do not decline either among the young (or among the old for that matter) or among those who have had the most education. There is then no sign that hope is evolving out of existence as part of some long-term process of "secularization."

Tiger informs us (*Optimism the Biology of Hope*, p. 21), "Optimists were more likely to cope and reproduce than pessimists, other things being equal; an important root of social cohesion and economic innovation is as biologically understandable as the sweating that accompanies fear, though far less tangible and immediate." He adds later (p. 35), "Thinking rosy futures is as biological as sexual fantasy. Optimistically calculating the odds is as basic a human action as seeking food when hungry or craving fresh air. . . . Making deals with uncertainty marks us as plainly as bipedalism." Even the most secular of ideologies, he contends, is infected by hope. "A restless certainty that however good or bad the experience is it can be better, routinely affects even the most thoroughgoing secularism."

17

McCready's data demonstrate that for some four-fifths of the population, Tiger's assertions are accurate enough. Most of us tend to hope.

2.2 *There also exists the need that this hope periodically be validated.*

Data on the meaning of the human condition are confusing. Evidence that our life is guided by nothing more than random, capricious chance is not completely persuasive, perhaps, but still persuasive. Furthermore, we experience sickness, suffering, tragedy, injustice, disappointment, frustration, and eventually and inevitably death. Hopefulness, thus, needs periodically to be reinforced or it would not be able to sustain the outrages of human existence. Tiger seems to miss this point completely. If the propensity to hope is a biological given, then along with it there must also be given a capacity to renew that hope. Such renewal is going to be required often in the course of life. If one is more modest than Tiger and merely postulates a powerful propensity to hope without claiming either universality or genetic programing, one must also postulate some kind of capacity—the exact nature of which can remain undefined—to periodically renew hopefulness. If hope were a given and did not have to be renewed, it is unlikely there would be religion. It is precisely because we need to renew our hopefulness that we have a propensity to engage in activities and behaviors that can be called "religious."

No specific evidence is required to sustain my second proposition since it is almost an inevitable consequence of the first. However, McCready's finding that hopefulness and optimism do not deteriorate offers confirmation if any is needed that hope is repeatedly renewed in the ordinary process of human life.

2.3 *In the human organism there is a capacity to find validation for hopefulness in a wide variety of experiences which are perceived as having been triggered by realities beyond the organism.*

At this stage of my discussion I do not wish to differentiate in any great detail among the "varieties of religious experiences," nor do I ask whether there is but one kind of hope experience and the differences among such experiences are merely matters of degree, or whether (as I suspect) there are varieties not only in intensity of hope experiences, but also varieties of kind.

Most serious investigators are willing to admit that intense religious experiences are widespread in the human race (even if, like many psychoanalytic writers on the subject, they write these experiences off as the "regression to childhood behavior pattern" or "quasi-regression"). The kinds of religious experiences described by William James—noetic, transcient, passive, ineffable—the experience of being lifted out of oneself and becoming one with a "higher power" have occurred to about one-third of the American population (and to approximately the same proportion of the English population). Research carried on by Sir Alister Hardy and Professor David Hay in England and by McCready and me in this country would indicate that the psychoanalysts are wrong; that, far from being quasi-schizophrenic, the modern mystics (about 35 percent of the population) tend to be paragons of mental health. But sick or well, deceived or visionary, the modern mystics—those who report the most intense sorts of experiences of hopefulness—are citizenry of advanced, industrial societies. It is worth reading some of the descriptions of these experiences to realize just how intense they are.

> I remember the night, and almost the very spot on the hilltop, where my soul opened out, as it were, into the In-

finite, and there was a rushing together of the two worlds, the inner and the outer. It was deep calling unto deep,—the deep that my own struggle had opened up within being answered by the unfathomable deep without, reaching beyond the start. I stood alone with Him who had made me, and all the beauty of the world, and love, and sorrow, and even temptation. I did not see Him, but felt the perfect unison of my spirit with His. The ordinary sense of things around me faded. For the moment nothing but an ineffable joy and exaltation remained. It is impossible fully to describe the experience. It was like the effect of some great orchestra when all the separate notes have melted into one swelling harmony that leaves the listener conscious of nothing save that his soul is being wafted upwards, and almost bursting with its own emotion. The perfect stillness of the night was thrilled by a more solemn silence. The darkness held a presence that was all the more felt because it was not seen. I could not any more have doubted that He was there than that I was. Indeed, I felt myself to be, if possible, the less real of the two. [Quoted in Greeley, *Death and Beyond*, 1976]

It happened in my room in Peterhouse on the evening of 1 February 1913, when I was an undergraduate at Cambridge. If I say that Christ came to me I should be using conventional words which would carry no precise meaning; for Christ comes to men and women in different ways. When I tried to record the experience at the time I used the imagery of the vision of the Holy Grail; it seemed to me to be like that. There was, however, no sensible vision. There was just the room, with its shabby furniture and the fire burning in the grate and the red-shaded lamp on the table. But the room was filled by a Presence, which in a strange way was both about me and within me, like light or warmth. I was overwhelmingly possessed by Someone who was not myself, and yet I felt I was more myself than I had ever been before. I was filled with an intense happiness, and almost unbearable joy, such as I had never known before and have never known since. And over all was a deep sense of peace and security and certainty. [Greeley, *Sociology of the Paranormal*, 1975, p. 44]

I had been ploughing all day in the black dust of the Lichtenburg roads, and had come very late to a place called the eye of Malmani—Malmani Oog—the spring of a river which presently loses itself in the Kalahari. We watered our horses and went supperless to bed. Next morning I bathed in one of the Malmani pools—and icy cold it was—and then basked in the early sunshine while breakfast was cooking. The water made a pleasant music, and near by was a covert of willows filled with singing birds. Then and there came on me the hour of revelation, when, though savagely hungry, I forgot about breakfast. Scents, sights, and sounds blended into a harmony so perfect that it transcended human expression, even human thought. It was like a glimpse of the peace of eternity. [Ibid., p. 46]

But, the experiences which refuel human hopefulness need not be so intense.

Fifty percent of a sample of young Americans have had experiences of being in touch with the "sacred," and 50 percent experience that there is order and purpose in their lives. When one combines ecstatic, sacred, and purpose experiences, more than 70 percent of young adults have had at least one of them, 20 percent report one of the other experiences several times, and 11 percent report them often. Nor is there any particular reason to think these three questions even begin to tap the hope-fulfilling experiences available to the human personality. Abraham Maslow's peak experiences were, according to his research, virtually universal in the young people with whom he worked. Ecstasy is not required for a hope experience. The theologian David Tracy has analyzed in considerable detail some of the "more secular" of hope experiences. Basic issues arise implicitly or explicitly, consciously or unconsciously, whenever we brush up against the stone wall that creates the boundary lines of our existence. When we push up against our own finite limits, we find ourselves wondering what human life means, and in that experience of finitude we obtain a hint of an explanation, a fleeting glimpse of an answer.

Scientists wonder where the imperatives come from that move them to work and discipline their efforts. Ethicians wonder why we have an overriding sense of moral obligation. A lover locked in passionate embrace, a mother wiping away the tears of her child, a tired and weary pilgrim refreshed by a clear spring morning, light breaking through the clouds, a parent or a spouse dies, a friendship ends in bitter quarrel—all these are or can be, in Father David Tracy's words, "limit-experiences." The scientist knows that his ethics can never reveal their ultimate source. The lovers understand that however strong the passion that unites them, they are still two separate persons, both are doomed to die; the mother perceives that these tears she can wipe away but that there will be others to fall later in life that no one will be able to wipe away. We cannot always help those we love and there will come a time when they will not be able to help us. Life is finite, and within the boundaries of life our own particular existence is hemmed in on all sides by physiological, biological, psychological, and sociological limitations. We may be pilgrims of the absolute, we may hunger for the infinite; but the being that we experience in our daily lives is all too fragile, all too finite.

And yet . . . and yet. . . . In such experiences of limitation we also may experience something more. The limit can become a horizon that not only defines where we are, but also suggests that there is something beyond where we are. In the limit-experience we bump up against the wall that imposes a boundary on our finite existence; but then, perhaps only for a fraction of a second, we find ourselves wondering why the wall is there, how we exist in relation to the wall. Is there something or perhaps even someone else on the other side? And every once in a while, in such horizon- or boundary-experiences, we have the impression that perhaps the wall moved a bit, or maybe we heard someone whispering on the other side of it.

The power of the limit-experience to "disclose" reality to us is in its power to stir up wonder. For we sense not merely the limitations on our existence, but the gratuity, the giftedness of that existence. And if existence is gratuitous and gifted, then it may also be gracious. And if there is graciousness, from whence does it come? The limit-experience, then, is a "religious experience" precisely in its capacity to stir up wonder in us. The scientists and the ethicians wonder about the imperatives that preside over their disciplines, the mother wonders about the marvel that is her child, the two lovers wonder how such great joy as is theirs can possibly be. Faced with the limitations on human affection and friendship, we wonder how friendship can be possible at all; and finally, pressed up against the wall of death we are still baffled by the phenomenon of life and by the refusal of life to give up hope even when we can see no farther than the wall of death.

The horizon-experience, then, is a revelation. It does not provide an "answer" to the agonized problems that our limitations impose upon us; it is a revelation in the sense that it is a "hint of an explanation"; it offers us a fleeting glimpse of possibility; it gives us a hint, sometimes subtle, almost imperceptible, and at other times powerful, that there is "something else" beyond the horizon. Religion, necessarily and inevitably, is about that "something else."

Such experiences are "rumors of angels," signals of the transcendent, or in David Tracy's more metaphysical words, "disclosive of a final, a fundamental, meaningfulness [which] bears a religious character."

These "disclosive" experiences reveal to us a world of meaning beyond the everyday, and this world is that through which religious symbols come. One might even say that it is a world out of which religious symbols explode. As Tracy notes: "Such a 'world,' by its strange ability to put us in touch with what we believe to be a final, a 'trustworthy,' meaning to our lives may also disclose to us, however hesitantly, the character of that ultimate horizon of meaning which religious persons call 'gracious,' 'eventful,' 'faith-full,' 'revelatory.' "

Limit-situations and limit-questions pose the fundamental religious issues, and, on occasion at least, they also suggest what the answers might be. Our thirst for self-transcendence—in scientific search, in moral and philosophical reflection, in celebration, in service, in love—runs up against Something Else (or Someone Else), which is perceived as having set boundaries to self-transcendence; and more than that, this Something Else is also perceived as responsible for both the self and the thrust for transcendence; or, alternately, it is the object of our longing for transcendence. It is perceived as having set a limit which is not permanent, as having created a stone wall that may eventually tumble down, as having drawn a boundary line, but a temporary one—or, to anticipate the theme of this book, it is perceived as a seductive lover, teasing us to go only so far but seeming also to promise that she (he) may be willing to give even more.

For the purposes of this book it is not necessary that one accept Tracy's theological conclusions. Yet, it is, I think, fair to say that his analytic description of what happens even in the secular experience of hope is accurate: we are given a hint of an explanation, even if the hint often seems inadequate, and in reflection is (or must be) judged as deceptive.

To have experienced grounds for hope, then, one need not undergo a profound and powerful experience such as described by William James and detailed in the previous quotations. We do not have to shout with Blaise Pascal,

> From about half past ten in the evening to
>   about half an hour after midnight.
>   Fire.
> God of Abraham, God of Isaac, God of Jacob,
> Not the God of philosophers and scholars.
> Absolute Certainty: Beyond Reason.

Joy. Peace.
Forgetfulness of the world and everything
    but God.
The world has not known thee,
    But I have known thee.
        Joy! joy! joy! tears of joy!

[Quoted by F.C. Happold, *Mysticism: A Study and
Anthology.* Middlesex England: Penguin Books Ltd.,
1964, a Pelican original, p. 39]

We need merely see a desert sunrise, the cold gleam of the sun
on a frozen lake on a winter morning, a happy smile on a
two-year-old, a touch of a friendly hand, the warmth or
reconciliation to both encounter our own limitations and also
encounter a hint of gratuity which *may* go beyond those
limitations. Not only do we have a capacity to renew our
hopefulness, but most of us seem to undergo at least intermit-
tent experiences which do, in fact, reinforce our hope, on occasion spectacularly.

2.4 *These experiences are perceived as an encounter with
goodness which exists in the realities that trigger them, but
which also in some fashion exist apart from or even beyond the
triggering realities.*

While there is no social science evidence which enables us
to fathom in precise detail the process of the experience that
reinforces hopefulness (though technically such research
could be designed and executed) there does exist a literature,
most of it philosophical or theological, which attempts to
describe the phenomenology of the hope experience. This
literature, not unreasonably, sees the experience as a
disclosure.

As Thomas Fawcett remarks, A disclosure of any kind is
only possible when something within a man's experience con-
fronts him in such a way that a response is evoked within

him. Trees, flowers, tiny animals are simply things; but when they are carried in a spring procession, they become a sign that spring has come. Even this really isn't a disclosure until the signs "produce specific reactions in us, [until] they operate at the personal level of emotion and imagination [and] something new appears to be given in the experience they create" (Greeley, *The Mary Myth*, 1977). The flowers, the tree branches, the animals are not merely a sign that spring is back, they have become a disclosure sign precisely because they create in us an experience of bumping up against the limits of the cosmos. The signs which announce spring speak of both death and life; the world is not dead, it constantly overcomes death. I see that sign; it forces me to consider my own death and discloses to me in one way or another that death is not ultimate. The thing has become a sign, and the sign in its turn, because it has evoked tough questioning and a tentative answer in me, has become a symbol.

Note well what has happened. The thing which has forced a limit-experience on me now becomes the symbol by which I interpret my experience and communicate it to others. This transformation of a thing into a limit-experience and a revelatory experience occurs, according to Fawcett, in three moments:

1. The presence of an existential need.
2. The moment of disclosure or perception itself.
3. The embodiment of the experience in symbolic form.

The existential need has to be there to begin with. There has to be some predisposition toward a limit-experience before the thing can produce such an experience. I can see the dune grass turn green every year and just remark to myself, "Well, it's spring again." Unless there is some need in a particular spring in the depths of my personality to wonder about the mysteries of life and death in the universe, the second and third steps of the limit-experience may not occur. I can encounter a beautiful woman on the street and experience nothing else than a slightly increased level of sexual fantasy unless there is some kind of powerful existential puzzling going on inside of me about the diversity of humankind and the baffling differentiation of that kind into male and female, a differentiation combined with an urge toward unity between male and female. Without the predisposition to wonder, all things, even the most exciting things, become commonplace. But, when the predisposition to wonder is there, then everything is potentially sacramental, and some things are overwhelmingly so.

Fawcett sees two phases in the process of a thing becoming a sacrament (my phrase, not his):

The Descent
1. The presence of an existential need;
2. The moment of disclosure or perception of need;
3. The symbolization of ontological anxiety.

The Ascent
1. The descent becomes the basis for further disclosure;
2. Creative disclosure or perception;
3. Symbolizations of integration and wholeness.

So I sit on the side of my dune with a need in the depths of my spirit (mostly unrecognized) to find some answer to the apparent chaos and absurdity of a human life that will surely be snuffed out in death. I then perceive that the dune grass is becoming green again; the grass is being reborn after a winter's death. "My God," I say (more in exclamation than in prayer). "The grass is reborn." It grows older without weakening, without becoming infirm. I too am growing older, but unlike the grass I move inevitably toward death. I have now symbolized my own ontological anxiety about death.

But I continue to stare at the grass. It seemed to be dead last November, but now it is alive again. Can it be that I am less important than the flowers of the field or the grass of the dune? I perceive that somehow, some way, life is stronger than death, that my life is stronger than my death. And so I celebrate the rebirth of the grass, the coming of spring, with a new sense of peace and serenity and wholeness. Life conquers death, and my life will ultimately conquer my death. Thus the symbol is transformed into limit-experience.

Or I encounter an extraordinarily beautiful woman. She is human like me but separate from me, distinct from me, not identifiable with me. I have been lonely, cut off, alienated, but have scarcely noted any existential need for union. In the experience of this beautiful woman, I perceive my alienation, my loneliness. It matters not whether I sleep with her. (The first person pronoun is used here in the general sense, *not* in any autobiographic sense.) Even if we do make love, the moment of union with her is fleeting, and I perceive in it that I really am not "at one" with her, that I am distinct, lonely, cut off. My ontological anxiety has now been symbolized in my relationship with that woman, and in its explicitness I am forced to probe more deeply into the dilemma of loneliness. But I also perceive that in the differentiation that comes from our separateness and distinctiveness there is also goodness, for she is tender and seductive and inspiring and gentle. She draws me out of myself both physiologically and psychologically. She discloses to me, and I perceive, that differentiation is a prelude to loving integration, and that which is separated can also be joined. If I feel cut off from myself, my friends, my world, from the ultimate forces that are at work in the universe, this woman becomes a sacrament to me that such divisions and separations and isolations can be transcended, and that differentiation is a prelude to wholeness.

Note that this experience of sexual differentiation can arise out of any encounter with a member of the opposite sex as long as there is a predisposing (perhaps unrecognized) existential need. The encounter can be the permanent relationship of a marriage or a chance passing on the street in which not a word is said. Note also that the experience of sexual differentiation, which is as commonplace as breathing, need not be sacramental. Sexual differentiation need not become a symbol; that it frequently has done so is beyond all doubt; that most of the time it does not become so in our lives is also beyond all doubt. Sex is not automatically a sacrament, but a lesson of human history is that it can easily become so.

What has happened in these two experiences? I have dealt with reality through an habitual structure of perceptions.

> The French philosopher Merleau-Ponty notes that humans organize and structure their experience simply because it is impossible to deal with an unstructured flow of consciousness. Such a structuring is a biological trait we have in common with the highest animals, though there is in humans, of course, in addition to the unconscious, biological structuring of experience, a conscious, reflective structuring. However, this latter builds on the former, which underpins and supports it. [Greeley, *The Mary Myth*, 1977, p. 26]

In my structured perceptions, dune grass and lovely women are parts of the environment, attractive and appealing in their own ways, doubtless, but quite ordinary and commonplace. But in these particular encounters a dialectic is set up between my existential needs and the revelatory power of the thing. Thus, between my yearnings for self-transcendence and the thing's unique and special capacity to reveal Being, the dialectic is established that reveals the pain of the limit-experience, consciously and explicitly hints that something beyond the experience may be perceived, and transforms the thing itself into symbol which embodies both my perception of the problem and my grasp of the hint of an answer.

Because of the dialectic that is set up, the ordinary structures of my perception have been shattered. The grass is no longer a green flora on my duneside; it rises in revolt, as it were, against such casual, structured perception and demands to be seen for what it is, a wondrous, marvelous splash of green which some playful spirit has tossed on my dune, perhaps as compensation for last year's erosion. "Look at me!" the grass screams. "See what I am! Learn from me about the Being which I reveal." The grass, then, shatters the structures of my perception and becomes a symbol which is a focus, a prism through which my perceptions are restructured. The grass serves three roles: it shatters my old perceptions, but only once I have agreed implicitly to the establishment of the dialectic; it reorganizes my perceptions into a new configuration; and it accompanies me as a symbol which will recall for me the experience I had on the dunes and enable me—if I am a poet—to share that experience with others.

Similarly, the woman also virtually screams at me (when my existential needs force me to be open to dialogue with her): "I am not merely part of the environment. I'm not part of the scenery. I am a person like you, but different. I am cut off and lonely like you, and in the difference between us lies the possibility of unity. In that unity we have together is the union of all things in whatever is ultimate." The woman, then, forces me to recognize my own "cut-offness;" she becomes a revelation of the potential unity of all things, and in that moment becomes a symbol—a symbol that does not cease to be a human person, of course. She remains a symbol around which I can organize my newly restructured perceptions of unity and diversity, of alienation and love. As a symbol, my relationship is not fleeting; she recalls to me my limit-experience of isolation and a hint of an explanation about unity that responded to that limit-experience. She not only has restructured my perceptions, she is a permanent reminder of that restructuring, and hence a guarantee that I will not slip back. Finally, should I be a poet or a novelist or a musician, she is a symbol through which I can communicate to others my limit-experience and the dazzling insight that comes from the shattering of old perceptions and the creations of new structures.

A limit-experience is essentially an experience of old perceptions being shattered and new ones being structured. It requires a dialogue between my existential need and the revelatory power of something else that shares the cosmos with me. At the core of the experience is the symbolization of that with which I am in dialogue. When, therefore, I speak to others of my experience, I necessarily fall back on the symbol because in one very real sense, the symbol is the experience.

Note that the symbolization of the thing, which is at the core of a limit-experience, is action-producing. I do not sit and look at the grass passively after it has intruded itself sacramentally into my life. I set out to work with a song on my lips (well, I would if I could sing!) and joy in my heart. Restructured perceptions lead to restructured living. One lives in response to the world one perceives; if one perceives the world differently, one lives differently. When I fall in love with a woman who reveals to me the existence of passionate tenderness in the cosmos, my behavior undergoes a transformation. I yearn to be with her, I sing about her, I praise her to all I know. If she is already mine and I am already hers, I desperately wish to make love with her precisely because of my experience of her as a valid and authentic "other." I experience a powerful yearning for unity. She has restructured my perceptions, and in the process she has inevitably changed my behavior.

We act, therefore, as a result of limit-experiences. The apostles experienced the risen Jesus, and then went forth and preached him. The nature lover sings, the lover makes love. The apostles preached for years before they wrote about it, and only then did they begin to turn to theology. One reflects on the symbol and its meaning only after one has lived—perhaps passionately—the renewed life the symbols have made possible. Reflection is derivative; action is primary. Reflection focuses on both the symbol and the subsequent action, and tries to explain to others—especially those to whom the symbol is not an effective means of communication—what the experience incarnated in the symbol and embodied in one's life really means.

It is technically possible to design social research which would examine the model of the hope experience described by Fawcett. Until the time at which such research is done one must be content with saying that the phenomenological description is plausible enough support for proposition 2.4.

2.5 *The goodness experience is perceived as overwhelming and yet ambiguous: good-but-mixed-with-ungood-but-still-good.*

There is no empirical social science evidence to support proposition 2.5. One must rely on the descriptions of those who have written about their own experiences or the philosophers who have tried to reflect on the phenomenology of these experiences. Some of those reporting on their experiences of hopefulness inform us that the ecstasy which they enjoyed was so overwhelming that evil is no longer important. But others, with perhaps more profound experiences, report that the "lover" (their choice of language) is like all lovers—ambiguous, unpredictable, erratic. There is joy and ecstasy for John of the Cross. There is also the dark night of the senses and the dark night of the soul.

For those who have more ordinary experiences of hope, the assertion that the experience does not eliminate the mixture of ambiguity and "ungoodness" may not need formal empirical confirmation because it seems to be so self-evident. The ordinary experience of hope does not eliminate the ambiguities from the human condition. On the contrary, precisely because an experience of limitation is more intensely perceived than under normal circumstances it may, indeed, heighten the ambiguity of the human condition. "Oh, slowly, slowly run you steeds of night," said the Roman poet Ovid in the arms of his lover. The experience of hope is often an experience of "hope against hope," of hope only marginally stronger than despair, of good only ever so slightly more powerful than evil.

It is again technically possible to design research which would document this proposition, should such documentation be required.

2.6 *The propensity to hope, the need for validation of hope, the capacity to experience goodness in external realities, and the perception of that goodness as ambiguous are all functions of that dimension of the organism which is called the prerational or the preconscious; these capacities and experiences are primarily a function of that aspect of the organism (brain?) in which free-floating images, pictures, stories exist independently of direct control by the conscious self.*

Proposition 2.6 is less a hypothesis to be empirically documented than an ordering of the previous five propositions. Religion, primordially defined as the result of experiences of hopefulness, occurs first of all in that dimension of our organism which might be called the "poetic."

Michael Polanyi, in the closing years of his remarkable life, wrote extensively on personal knowledge or tacit knowledge; that is, the deeply insightful, intuitive cognition that we have about things before we "know" them in any self-conscious and explicit fashion. According to Polanyi, our great discoveries come not as clearly thought-out answers, carefully prepared questions based on theoretical consideration according to the standard format of the "scientific method." On the contrary, the great insights, the paradigm-shattering ones, to use the phrase of Thomas Kuhn, come before the answers and even before the questions. At some deep level in our personalities we intuit the truth about reality, and then, under the influence of this intuition, seek to ask the questions that will enable us to "surface" our insight as an articulated answer to the questions. This description of personal knowledge flies in the face of all we learned in our high school and college textbooks about scientific method.

Claude Lévi-Strauss, in his discussions of symbolic myths, speaks of the French "artistic game" of bricollage. The artist or craftsman, working with a limited set of components—some string, a few rocks, some pieces of wood, some bits of wire—assembles, demolishes, and then reassembles constructs which can represent as many different things as his playful imagination wants to make them represent. Lévi-Strauss suggests that the myth makers operate in the same way. They have a limited number of images, pictures, metaphors, stories, symbols, and they endlessly rearrange, reconstruct, reorder their component parts into similar and yet diverse myths much like our dreams rearrange the experiences of our waking conscious life. It is clear that tellers of folk tales enjoy tremendous liberty in manipulating their limited resources to make many different, though not unrelated points about the meaning of the human condition. Homer, for example, must have relied on a vast collection of divergent folk tales which in a work of sheer genius he wove into a seamless web. In Irish mythology the tales of Finn Mac-Cool and of Queen Maeve are by no means part of a single well-integrated story (though sometimes attempts were made in the old sagas to force the divergent tales together), but are rather the creations of different story tellers with different goals and purposes.

The same bricollage phenomenon is at work in both the Jewish and Christian scriptures. The book of Tobit, for example, is clearly composed of a number of folk tales and folk images that were "lying around" for the teller of the tale, just as the pieces of string and wire and wood were "lying around" in a French farmyard. More importantly, the late apocalyptic literature of the Second Temple era was put together in substantial part by reweaving the Creation myths to be found in Genesis, which certainly existed long before the writing of Genesis, in Hebrew folk mythology. So too even in the Christian scriptures there is no single account of the death of Jesus and then his followers' experience of him as still alive, but many different tales and traditions have emerged making rather different points out of the manipulation of the various components of pictures and stories.

Mihaly Czikszentmihalyi has developed the notion of "flow" to describe certain "peak" experiences of altered or quasi-altered states of consciousness. It is the nature of "flow" experience to push our talents and our skills to their outer limits, but not beyond that limit. The chess player faced with a difficult opponent, but one with whom he is well matched; the surgeon, performing intricate operations that are just inside the limits of his abilities; the skier, performing a tricky slope that he knows he can master; the quarterback, "reading" the defensive secondary—all these experience "flow" states. Their disciplined, highly trained, carefully polished skills react quickly, automatically, smoothly, responding with casual decisiveness to every slight movement in the situation. It is as though the skills themselves take over and direct the person involved. John Brody, who once tossed a football for the San Francisco '49ers, described such an experience as a "slow motion" drama in which he could see his responses with the slowly unfolding defensive patterns even before he had responded. His skills as quarterback, in other words, "told him" what to do without his having to devote any conscious thought to the problem of, let us say, a free safety, leaving his position and crossing the field. Similarly, trial lawyers—or anyone else who must think on his/her feet—often describe their responses in critical situations as words they never would have "thought" of themselves if they had time. The words just came, they "flowed" out of them. What exactly goes on in this altered state of consciousness? What is the nature of this "creative" process? Does a muse, indeed, take over and whisper in our ear, as some varieties of Platonic philosophy once suggested? Today that seems an absurd question, and yet, the poet, the artist, the painter, I think, will all testify that they do "hear" voices or do "see" visions. The model of a "muse" nicely subsumes the data.

The creative process, in other words, seems to be something intellectual, but intellectual in a quite different way than our ordinary thought process is intellectual. Aristotle postulated an "active" or "agent" intellect, a dimension of the human personality, if you will, which not only received knowledge, but actively "went out" to order the components from which knowledge would come. The Islamic Aristotelians in Spain in the early middle ages were so impressed by the power of this "intellectus agens" that they suggested that there was but a single such intellect for the whole human race in which we all participated—a construct not at all unlike, when push comes to shove, the Platonic muse. Most Platonists and some Aristotelians, then, were so impressed with the power that takes over in the altered state of consciousness called creativity that they placed this power outside the human personality. Thomas Aquinas, the stable, sensible Neapolitan that he was, dismissed such a notion, and the creative intellect was put back where it belonged—solidly within the personality of the ordinary individual—even if it was still seen as a spark of some higher Creativity.

If, therefore, creativity is neither in the daily consciousness, nor in the Freudian unconsciousness, nor in some Platonic or Aristotelian hyperconsciousness, where else is it? One runs out of prefixes and ends up with the notion of the preconscious. In the last several decades two very different individuals developed from very different traditions the notion of the preconscious intellect as the locus of human creativity: the psychoanalyst Lawrence Kubie and the Thomistic philosopher Jacques Maritain (in the A. W. Mellon

Lectures in the Fine Arts at the National Gallery of Arts). This strange convergence of the psychoanalyst and the philosopher—of which the two men were apparently totally unaware—is a fascinating phenomenon, and while convergence does not "prove" the existence of a preconscious intellect, it does lend some plausibility to the model.

Be it noted, by the way, that one is dealing here with a model, a postulate to explain phenomena, rather than a clearly proven dimension of the human personality.

First let us listen to Lawrence Kubie. He places the preconscious of the human personality between the rational and the unconscious.

There is, however, another type of mentation whose relationship to its roots is figurative and allegorical. The function of this intermediate form of mentation is to express at least by implication the nuances of thought and feeling, those collateral and emotional references which cluster around the central core of meaning. Here every coded signal has many overlapping meanings; and every item of data from the world of experience has many coded representatives. This is the form of coded language which is essential for all creative thinking, whether in art or science. Therefore, we will have much more to say about it below. In technical jargon, this second type of symbolic process is called *preconscious.*

. . . On the conscious level he [a scientist] deals with them as communicable ideas and approximate realities. On the *preconscious* level he deals with swift condensations of their multiple allegorical and emotional import, both direct and indirect. On the *unconscious* level, without realizing it, he uses his special competence and knowledge to express the conflict-laden and confused levels of his own spirit, using the language of his specialty as a vehicle for the outward projection of his own internal struggles. Since this happens without his knowledge, it is a process which even in his own field can take over his creative thinking, distorting and perverting it to serve his unconscious needs and purposes, precisely as happens in a dream or in the symptom formations of neurotic and psychotic illness. [*Neurotic Distortion of the Creative Process*, pp. 30–32]

Caught as it is between ordinary waking consciousness and the unconscious, the preconscious is in trouble.

> Preconscious processes are assailed from both sides. From one side they are nagged and prodded into rigid and distorted symbols by unconscious drives which are oriented away from reality and which consist of rigid compromise formations, lacking in fluid inventiveness. From the other side they are driven by literal conscious purpose, checked and corrected by conscious retrospective critique. The uniqueness of creativity, i.e., its capacity to find and put together something new, depends on the extent to which preconscious functions can operate freely between these two ubiquitous concurrent and oppressive prison wardens. [p. 45]

Finally, Kubie believed that the preconscious exercise of creativity is essentially a matter of seeing new relationships—a bricollage exercise, in other words.

> It is, I believe, a fair generalization to state quite simply that although the uncovering of new facts and of new relationships among both new and old data is not the whole of creativity, it is the essential process without which there can be no such thing as creativity. Consequently, creativity implies *invention*; e.g., the making of new machines or processes by the application of old or new facts and principles or a combination of them in order to uncover still newer facts and newer combinations, and to synthesize new patterns out of data whose interdependence had hitherto gone unnoted and unused. It is this which is common to all creativeness, whether in music as described by Mozart, or in painting as described by Delacroix and others, or in poetry as described by Paul Valery, A. E. Housman, etc., or in science as pointed out by Gregg, Claude Bernard, Richard Tolman, Richet, and other scientists. [p. 50]

Incidentally, later in the book Kubie compares preconscious activity to that of music—a comparison that he, without realizing it, has in common with both Plato and Maritain: "The extraordinary power of preconscious condensation is often demonstrated by a single thought which reverberates through the mind like a haunting melody" (p. 73).

Now to turn to Jacques Maritain. Creativity, "art," as Maritain calls it, is a "habitus, an inner quality or stable and deep rooted disposition that raises the human subject and his natural powers to a higher degree of vital formation and energy, making him possessed of a particular strength of his own . . . a master quality, an inner demon if you prefer —has developed in us . . . " (pp. 48–49). Creativity, then, is, or at least involves, first of all the disciplined skill. Nor is it to be found either outside the human personality or in the depths of the human unconscious. It is in "neither the surrealist inferno nor the Platonic heaven. I think that what we have to do is to make the Platonic Muse descend into the soul of man, where she is no longer Muse, but creative intuition; and Platonic inspiration descend into the intellect united with imagination . . . [nor] is it a purely unconscious activity . . . but, rather . . . an activity which is *principally* unconscious, but, the point of which emerges into consciousness. Poetic intuition, for instance, is born in the unconscious, but it emerges from it; the poet is not unaware of this intuition, on the contrary it is his most precious light and the primary rule of his virtue. . . . But, he is aware of it . . . on the *edge* of the unconscious" (pp. 90–91; author's italics).

Maritain concludes:

> There are two kinds of unconscious, two great domains of psychological activity screened from the grasp of consciousness: the preconscious of the spirit in its living springs, and the unconscious of blood and flesh, instincts, tendencies, complexes, repressed images and desires, traumatic memories, as constituting a closed or autonomous

dynamic whole. I would like to designate the first kind of unconscious by the name of *spiritual* or, for the sake of Plato, *musical* unconscious or preconscious; and the second by the name of *automatic* unconscious or *deaf* unconscious—deaf to the intellect, and structured into a world of its own apart from the intellect; we might also say, in quite a general sense, leaving aside any particular theory, *Freudian unconscious.* [pp. 91–92; author's italics]

Note how almost miraculously similar are the comments of Maritain and Kubie, even in the reference to music. Maritain insists that this creative activity is an activity of reason, but he defines reason to include something much broader than ordinary waking consciousness. (Incidentally, Maritain has a diagram on page 108 of his book, and Kubie, on page 40, which are strikingly similar in their contents, if not in their graphics.)

> Reason does not only consist of its conscious logical tools and manifestations, nor does the will consist only of its deliberate conscious determinations. Far beneath the sunlit surface thronged with explicit concepts and judgments, words and expressed resolutions or movements of the will, are the sources of knowledge and creativity, of love and suprasensuous desires, hidden in the primordial trans-lucid night of the intimate vitality of the soul. Thus, it is that we must recognize the existence of an unconscious or preconscious which pertains to the spiritual powers of the human soul and to the inner abyss of personal freedom, and of the personal thirst and striving for knowing and seeing, grasping and expressing; a spiritual or musical unconscious which is specifically different from the automatic or deaf unconscious. [p. 94]

Maritain goes beyond Kubie to give a name to the functioning preconscious. He calls it the Agent Intellect or the Illuminating Intellect. It is that part of our personality which analyzes and decomposes reality outside. It serves it up for the consideration of our conscious, rational, discursive mind.

It is "a merely active and perpetually active intellectual energy . . . which permeates the images with its pure and purely activating spiritual life and actuates or awakens the potential intelligibility which is contained in them" (p. 97). It is that energy which operates on the images gathered by our senses, drawing the intelligible content from these images. The Illuminating Intellect is spiritual sun ceaselessly radiating, which activates everything in intelligence, and whose light causes all our ideas to arise in us, and whose energy permeates every operation of our mind. And this primal source of light cannot be seen by us; it remains concealed in the unconscious of the spirit" (pp. 98–99).

Maritain suggests that the preconscious—the locus of creativity—is in fact a ceaselessly operating intellectual energy which is an essential part of the human act of knowing. Our images can either be in the automatic unconscious of Freud or in the spiritual preconscious; and it is precisely insofar as they are in the spiritual preconscious that they present the raw material of creativity. For those of you who may be tempted to dismiss Maritain as a reactionary Thomist, one can only point out that he is saying virtually the same thing as is the American psychoanalyst Lawrence Kubie, both the source of creativity is a "scanning mechanism" locked in the depths of the human personality, but operating beyond the depths, ceaselessly exploring like a searchlight radar antenna, the world outside, and "locking on" to that world through the pictures and images it uncovers. The creative activity of the preconscious, freed temporarily from the constraint of literal reason, "takes over," releases our deeply intuitive personal knowledge, activates the smooth flow of our skills, and rearranges the components with which we are playing.

It is in the process something like this that I am suggesting that the religious imagination produces the symbols which resonate with the reality that has been experienced. Obviously, at the present state of our knowledge it is impossible

41

empirically to test at least directly such an assumption. However, as will be seen later on in this book, propositions based on the assumption do, indeed, stand up to empirical validation.

2.7 *Almost any external reality is capable of triggering an experience that will reinforce hope; certain realities because of their power and importance are especially likely to do so — sun, water, night, mountains, fire, birth, sexual differentiation, food, drink, etc. The language which wells up out of our "creative imagination" which articulates our experience with these realities is likely to be as ambiguous as the experience itself.*

A. Almost any reality is capable of producing hope.

This subproposition scarcely needs confirmation for anyone who has read much of world religious literature.

B. Some reality either because of genetic and biological programing (Carl Sagan) or because of the "structure of the human personality" (Mircea Eliade) is especially likely to trigger experiences of hope.

This subproposition is richly documented in the literature of the history of religions; for example, in such a volume as Mircea Eliade's *Patterns of Comparative Religion.*

For the purpose of this book it does not seem necessary to inquire, for example, whether humans are genetically programed to find reinforcement for their hope in a sacred meal, or whether there is some deep preconscious or unconscious dynamism in the human personality which inclined us to intermittently renew our hopefulness—either deliberately or undeliberately—through a "special" meal. It seems to suffice to say that eating and drinking are so overwhelmingly important in the human condition and that eating and drinking with those one loves are so pleasurable (some of the time) that it would take major effort to exclude hope-renewing experiences from eating and drinking.

C. The language which describes hope experiences is ambiguous.

The third subproposition needs more discussion. One
must establish here that necessarily and inevitably the
language which flows from limit-experiences is a different
kind of language than language we use at other times—a
much more poetic and playful language, as Sten Stenson has
observed.

Limit-experience, like my encounter with the woman on
the street, is not a neat, orderly, unambiguous, simple reality. The thing which reveals itself to us reveals itself in its full-
ness; it is dense, multilayered, polyvalent. It says many things
to me simultaneously; some of them are paradoxical, some of
them even contradictory. One who has fallen in love knows
full well that no set of logical propositions is adequate to
describe the complexity, the paradox of the beloved. One
tries to say everything at once and ends up babbling. All
things are complicated, and those things which are most
likely to be sacramental are especially so. To attempt to
describe just one aspect of the symbol is to risk distorting the
symbol substantially by neglecting its other aspects. I
describe the seriousness and intelligence of my loved one, but
having done that, I may make her sound terribly dull because
I have not had an opportunity to simultaneously describe her
humor and playfulness.

So it is with limit-experiences and the language we use to
describe them. It is not merely that such language is "odd," as
Ian Ramsey says. If one is speaking of limit-experience, one
must use special language simply because limit-experiences
are different from the ordinary experiences for which ordinary language is appropriate. You do not describe an event
in which a thing becomes a symbol in ordinary prose; you
must fall back on metaphor, parable, paradox; you must in-
troduce a "qualifier," as Ramsey says, which indicates to the
listener or the reader that you are now using words in their
limit-sense and not in their ordinary sense.

Of its nature, limit-language involves tension. The two terms of the metaphor which is latent in limit-language must be in some tension if they are to produce the startling and perception-shattering experience in the listener which religious language is designed to produce. Such statements as "the first shall be last, the last shall be first," "he is dead but has risen," and "she is a mother but a virgin" represent limit-language use of words—words used to convey limit-experiences. Paul Ricoeur says that the language we use to describe the limit-experience, which a symbol both creates and attempts to repeat, goes to the limits of language. The language of religion does not so much deny the ordinary as it intensifies it. In Father Tracy's words, it is "an intensification of the everyday." The unexpected happens; a strange world of meaning is projected which challenges, jars, disorients our everyday visions precisely by both showing us the limits to the everyday and projecting the limit character of the whole.

Limit-language, then, is designed to convey a limit-experience, to convert a thing into a symbol. It is language designed to make the symbol "explode with a linguistic power that discloses possibilities for human existence which seem and are beyond the limit of what our ordinary language and experience might imagine" (*The Mary Myth*).

Such writers as Dominic Crossen and David Tracy have shown that the very language of the Gospel parables has been designed to establish tension, to cut through existing structures of perception with the sharp knife of paradox. There is tension built into, for example, the juxtaposition of the words "good" and "Samaritan," or "first" and "last," which, even before we hear the stories, catch us by surprise and set us to wondering. Both in their substance and in their language the parables are paradoxical, shattering, exploding, and disclosing narratives. Every child, and the child in every one of us, is ready to plead, "Tell me a story." For the role of stories is to explain life, and the good stories, in their very substance and in the structure of their language, become revelation. In the shattering, disturbing, confusing, and challenging parables of the Gospel we are confronted with "one possible mode of being in the world: to live with explicit faith, with complete trust, with unqualified love." The story asks us to consider the possibility that we can live a life of fundamental trust, confidence, and total commitment to the goodness which has exploded out of the story and is seeking to take possession of us.

Thus, attempts to persuade others to perceive a thing as a symbol result in necessarily odd, unusual, and apparently bizarre language. The explanation of symbols cannot be made to fit the dimensions of ordinary discourse precisely, because it is concerned with shattering forms and structures of everyday perceptions and the discourse that may flow from it. But symbols and the language that attempts to describe them are ambiguous in a second sense also.

When a thing becomes a symbol, it speaks to us all at once, and much of what it has to say we hear very dimly indeed. When we describe our experience to someone else, when we attempt to produce in him the same shattering and restructuring of perceptions that occurred in our experience, when we try to turn the thing into a symbol for him, it is altogether possible that the experience which is produced in him will enable him to see something in the symbol that we did not see. Suppose I write a poem about my dune grass. I have not heard clearly everything the grass has to say, but if my poem produces a similar experience in someone who reads it, he may not hear everything I have heard but he may also hear something that was really there when the grass spoke to me, but which I missed completely. In reading my poem he searches not so much, or at least not entirely, for the meaning behind my words, which I have designed to convey the kind of experience the grass produced in me. He also, and perhaps more importantly, is trying to find the meaning "in front" of the words; that is, what does the grass say to him when it has produced in him through the mediation of my words an experience similar to mine of a thing becoming a symbol. For example, I may not have noticed that thin, apparently weak roots of the dune grass indeed hold my great and mighty dune together, and if it were not for the grass, wind and rain and snow would wreak havoc with my dune (assuming the lake waves should leave it alone). Like me, the reader of my imaginary poem experiences the limit-situation of the death and rebirth of nature, but he also experiences an aspect of that rebirth which is truly there but which I may have only dimly perceived or missed completely—the powerful binding force of a reborn nature which holds the potentially disintegrating inanimate reality together. (And, of course, he thereby perceives all kinds of ecological implications of my experience, which I either missed or only vaguely sensed.)

He is not distorting my experience; he is not reading into it something that is not there; he is having the same experience I did (or one very similar) through the mediation of my words. He is perceiving something deep and latent in the ontological reality of the experience that I missed.

Similarly, I may know a woman for years and suddenly discover an aspect of her personality that hitherto had been shrouded in mystery. Indeed, if I am not constantly discovering new things about her, our life together has become dull and routine. It is not that I am reading something into our experience together that was not there; nor is it that she suddenly becomes someone she was not before. This aspect of her selfhood was always there and was always speaking to me, but our dialogue has only today developed to such a stage that I perceive her speaking to me about this aspect of her personality. I am not "getting behind" the meaning of our original experience of each other; rather, I am now "in front of" that experience and seeing in it something I never saw before.

It is a phenomenon something like this that Paul Ricoeur has in mind when he speaks of the "prospective" sense of a text. When one searches for the "prospective" meaning of a symbol, one does not ask merely or even principally what he who first articulated that symbol within a specific religious tradition perceived consciously or explicitly; one asks, rather, what illumination we are able to receive from experiencing the thing-turned-symbol or the problem of being-in-the-world as we experience them given our situation, our information, and our insights today? If we permit the thing-turned-symbol to shatter our perspectives as it shattered the perspectives of its author, and then go on to reorganize our perspectives, what new structures of perception emerge for us? Can the limit-experience that he produces in us through the language by which he describes his experience give us illumination from the thing-turned-symbol that he missed, dimly perceived, or, in fact, could not perceive within the context of the time and place of his experience?

Metaphors, symbols, myths are open-ended. No limits can be set, notes Ian Barbour, to how far the comparison in such a figure of speech can be extended, because it has an unspecifiable number of potentialities for articulation left for the hearer or the reader to explore. "It is not an illustration of an idea already explicitly spelled out, but a suggestive invitation to the discovery of further similarities" (*Myths, Models, and Religion*, p. 14). It is precisely because a symbol (like a parable) is open-ended that it can be extended to new situations. The symbol presents a comparison to be explored, insights to be discovered, a many-faceted flow of images to be enjoyed. It illumines one's situation so that one sees aspects of reality which one might otherwise have missed; and at the same time the contact with a newly illumined reality can reflect back on the symbol itself and enable one to discover a potential extension of the basic comparison that was hitherto unperceived.

The first of the three subpropositions, as I remarked, is so evident as to hardly need proof, though one supposes that it could be empirically documented by extensive content analysis of religious works, particularly descriptions of religious experiences. The second subproposition has been richly validated by the research in comparative religions (or the history of religions as this subdiscipline is now commonly called). The third subproposition has been adequately validated by those like Stensen, Fawcett, and Tracy who have studied religious language, though not so convincingly that their adversaries are willing to concede that religious language ought not to be the same as the language of science and historical scholarship. Since I take the position that primordially religion is a function of the creative imagination I must side with those who contend that if religious language follows the same rules as those imposed on the language of historical scholarship, it ceases to be religious. My position is probably a matter of definition and cannot be either proven or defended, though I shall endeavor to explain and develop it subsequently in this book.

2.8 *In addition to being perceived as ambiguous and overwhelming, the goodness which is encountered in experiences which reinforce hope is perceived as mystifying, fascinating, terrifying, and hilarious.*

Rudolf Otto, in his book *The Holy*, asserts that the sacred or the "totally other" is both "tremendens" and "fascinosa," terrifying and fascinating; one wants to run from it in fear, and yet stay behind to examine it more closely, indeed, even surrender oneself completely to it. Both the terror and the fascination arise from the fact that the Other is, indeed, other—that is, totally different from us, and yet in some ways not completely dissimilar from us.

Paradoxically we often also find ourselves driven toward hilarity in our encounters with the Other: Laughter sweeps a group of monks over some minor imperfection in ceremonial, the most solemn of dances and songs are burlesqued, the sacred feast degenerates into an orgy. Perhaps it is all a matter of whistling in the dark as we go by the graveyard. Perhaps we laugh to relieve our tensions. Perhaps we find the game of religious ritual, like all games, ultimately ridiculous. Perhaps we burst into laughter to escape the unbearable tension of being too close to the Other.

It is again technically feasible to explore the terror, the fascination, and the laughter of religious experiences. To be logically correct, therefore, proposition 2.8 should be understood as predicting that some people at some times will have experiences of hopefulness that are mystifying, fascinating, terrifying, and hilarious.

2.9 *Implicit in the experience of hope is the possibility of "salvation." Religious groups which do not confirm that possibility or sufficiently emphasize it run the risk of losing some of their members to other groups that do.*

The first part of proposition 2.9 is merely a logical conclusion from the previous proposition, so long as "salvation" is understood to mean a process by which that for which we hope can be achieved. Even the most secular ideology, Tiger's among others, does indeed promise salvation—the "classless society," or "self-fulfillment," or "living in harmony with nature." Salvation in the context of this chapter merely means the continued pursuit of that which is revealed in the experience of hope.

The phenomenon of humans turning away from established groups in times of stress or crisis or frustration to seek "salvation" from new religious movements has been amply documented by historical scholars (see, for example, Peter Worsley's *The Trumpet Shall Sound* or Norman Cohn's *In Pursuit of the Millennium*). Hope and salvation are the raw "stuff" out of which religion is made. When established religions lose interest in salvation, other, usually new groups emerge to preach salvation. Thus, the phenomenon of the growth of religious cults in the United States in the 1970s may very well have resulted from the fact that many of the main-line denominations are more concerned with religious institutional problems or with social action commitments than they are with hope and salvation, and that many of their members—for whatever reason (geographic mobility, political disillusionment, social unease)—experience a heightened need to have their hope reinforced and to have the path of the message of salvation explicated. It is, of course, quite possible to discover whether those Americans—particularly young Americans—who presently find the cults so attractive are refugees from main-line denominations and have high needs for a reinforcement of hope and the assurance of salvation.

In this chapter I have used the word "hope" to describe both the human disposition to believe, as Tiger puts it, that the odds are not altogether unfavorable and the experiences which reinforce that disposition. There can be other names for the experiences—limit-experiences, horizon experiences, religious experiences, experiences of giftedness, experiences of gratuity. A common name in the Western World for such experiences is "grace." While the word has acquired technical theological connotations which may make it ambiguous, I nonetheless propose it henceforth in this book to describe experiences that reinforce the human propensity to hope.

All but one of the propositions are empirically testable and many of them already can be confirmed from data existing in one or the other scholarly disciplines: humans hope; their hope is reinforced and renewed by some of their experiences. Both the hope and the experience principally are to be found in the human creative imagination. The language which springs from the preconscious to articulate and resonate such experiences is as ambiguous and prerational as is the experience itself.

Just as there is a wide "variety" of grace experiences so there is in all likelihood a wide variety of needs for and propensities to hope influenced by biological, psychological, biographical, and cultural resources that humans bring to their life experiences. Thus, we can conclude this chapter with one testable proposition which will subsume most of the others: *The greater a person's propensity to hope and his need to hope and his capacity to experience renewals of hope, the more likely that person is to be in some sense of the word "religious."*

Chapter Three
Symbols and Stories

Thus far I have argued that religion primordially is based on the experience of grace, a grace which renews the human propensity to hope, and that the renewing experience takes place in the preconscious or the "creative imagination." Note that nothing is said thus far about "God" or the "supernatural." We are dealing at this level of our theorizing with raw experience, the sort of experience in which one may act, but about which one has yet to reflect.

3.1 *A symbol is a picture or an image which resonates and articulates and re-presents the experience of grace. It also may be used to share this experience with others by re-presenting to the others parallel experiences of their own.*

The first proposition is a matter of definition, though it has been distilled from the work of literary critics and philosophers who are engaged in analysis of metaphor as symbol. My image of the dune grass or of the woman in the street presented in the last chapter now exists in my preconscious as a residue of my experiences of these realities. As images of spring and sexual differentiation they can rearticulate, re-present, and renew for me that original experience, and, perhaps, expand and enrich, as I am scarcely the only one in humankind who has been renewed in hope by spring or by a beautiful woman. I can use my images which are residues of those experiences to share the experience with others, either unself-consciously or quite self-consciously— should I, for example, attempt to write a poem about either event. Note that I do not impose my experience on others. Indeed, I cannot do so. I must, rather, reach into the raw material of their preconscious to stimulate such raw materials so that the others recall parallel experiences of their own and, perhaps, resonate more deeply their own experiences because they have shared mine.

While this proposition is definitional, it is part of a link of propositions around which I have organized this third chapter and which can be validated empirically (and which I shall point out shortly have been validated empirically) by examining the role of religious imagery in persons' lives.

3.2 *The experience of grace promises salvation by validating the purposefulness of human life: our existence is not a series of random, unconnected events. It has, rather, a beginning, a middle, and a conclusion.*

This proposition is a logical explication of understandings inherent in several previous propositions. Hope means that there is a future, just as there has been a past and there is a present. In the past are the beginnings of my life. In the present is the middle, and in the future there is that for which I hope, "salvation," or whatever I may call it, if, indeed, I call it anything at all. It is the essence of hope that this past, present, and future be thought of as having some purpose, however vague, however confused, however ill-defined. I am coming from somewhere—I may not quite know where—and I am going somewhere—again I may not know where. Spring on the dunes points back to other springs as well as forward to the possibility of yet more renewing rebirth. Perhaps it suffices for hope that the future holds at least the promise of more renewals. Similarly, the lovely woman recalls loving in-timacies of the past and implies that such intimacies are not yet finished. Perhaps it is enough for there to be hope for one to experience the promise that there will be more loving in-timacies.

Observe that these experiences can be utterly secular. There is no need for an explicit or conscious ecclesiastical or "transcendental" linkage. Spring and an attractive member of the opposite sex renew my confidence that all is not yet finished.

3.3 Implicit in the experience of grace is the linking of a story of an individual with a Great Story. The meaning of the in-dividual life is related to the overarching Meaning of the Cosmos.

Just as I have a beginning, a middle, and a conclusion, so the cosmos of which I am a part has a beginning, a middle, and a conclusion. It has a story and I have a story, and my experience of grace links these stories. I need not reflect at any great length or even explicitly on that linkage. It is pres-ent in the experience of grace. The renewal of spring each year is part of the movement of the stars across the heavens; the body of the beautiful girl is part of the process of the con-tinuation of the species. In my grace experiences I perceive both as benign processes, continuing Life, and I experience myself as Involved in that continuation of life. I am part of creation and I am capable of the experience of re-creation. In-deed, I am caught up, immersed, swept along by the process of creation, both being re-created myself, and creating others. As will be noted later in the book, the relationship be-tween the Story and some of the more practical dimensions of our behavior can be quite powerful (our sexual life and our political involvement, for example).

3.4 *Creation and renewal images are fundamental responses to the experience of grace. When religious groups lose such images, many of their members tend to turn elsewhere for images of creation and re-creation.*

The works of Charles Long and Joseph Campbell leave little doubt about the virtual universality of creation mythology among human people. Such myths serve to provide an explanation for the cosmos and an opportunity for the individual to link his own purposes with the purpose of the cosmos. In these mythologies, creation is almost always perceived as the imposition of order on chaos (Mircea Eliade), a position that gives the ordered universe—cosmos—a tenuous victory over the disordered universe—chaos. Purposefulness defeats chance, but in most creation mythologyies only just barely. The creation stories normally, as Eliade points out, are presented in such a way that the person who hears them is able not merely to subsume his own story under the creation story, but actually to share in the of that story, to join in the process of imposing order on chaos, purpose on chance, direction on confusion.

Such elaborate creation mythologies, of course, go far beyond the usually implicit "cosmology" that the individual person senses in his experience of grace. The individual experience merely reveals symbolically a renewing process of which the individual is a part. The great creation myths, however, have the religious power they do precisely because they flow from and can readily be linked back to individual experience. When established religions lose track of their own creation and renewal myths, then secular renewal cosmology, millennialistic movements, messianic cults, and political revolutionary creeds intervene to promise the destruction of the old and the creation of the new. Some humans have greater need for renewal experience and renewal symbols than others, and sometimes these symbols may be more important than others (in both the lives of individuals and the lives of communities). But the attraction of renewal symbols is powerful, precisely because it is the possibility of renewal which grace reveals.

3.5 *The images, then, which re-present and resonate and articulate experiences of grace are stories linking my story to a cosmic story, linking the purpose of my life to Higher Purposes.*

All grace-produced symbols are stories. For the purposes of this book it is possible to leave aside the question of whether all metaphors are implicit narratives. The grace-produced symbol is, however, certainly a narrative, precisely because it is both the result and the cause of a renewal of hope. It is a story linking my story to the Great Story. Hence, grace-produced symbols of hope are not static images (if any image in the human preconscious could be static), but dynamic, moving images which "tell me a story." Nathan Scott argues that the plea of a little child, "Mommy, tell me a story," is, in fact, a "wild prayer of longing," and David Tracy, quoting a line from Wallace Stevens, calls it a "blessed rage for order." The little child more explicitly and more self-consciously than the rest of us wants a story that will clarify reality for him.

In their most simple, fundamental, and primordial form, these stories are not elaborate or developed. They have a motion dynamic, a thrust, and a direction not merely because experiences of grace orient us toward action, but because they reveal a continuing action. The experience of grace is the experience of an ongoing story, and the grace symbol resonates, represents, and articulates that ongoing story.

The raw materials of this story lay scattered about in our preconscious, as Claude Lévi Strauss observes, just as do the raw materials of bricollage lay strewn about a French farmyard. The creative imagination rearranges these raw materials to most effectively rearticulate the renewing experience of grace.

There are just so many components strewn about our creative imagination which can be assembled to represent the experience of a beautiful member of the opposite sex or the beginning of spring. The art of the storyteller or the minstrel consists of rearranging these components to convey his/her unique experience, and, thus, represent to others the unique aspects of their own experience that they have not hitherto perceived. Each of us is a storyteller and a poet, at least for ourselves, though we may expend little time or energy on such exercises (or perhaps, more precisely, we may pay little attention to what actually goes on in our creative preconscious).

I have been told (in personal conversation) that some of those working with computerized artificial intelligence have found it useful to simulate human performance through a series of "scenarios." They contend that it is useful to model human intelligence as having on file little "skits" which we act out routinely in the appropriate situations—such as entering a restaurant. These skits or scenarios might be thought of as constituting together the "drama" of at least a segment of our lives.

It is not merely useful, then, to conceptualize a person's behavior as being part of a story in which he is both the narrator and the principal actor. It may also be true, and more basically and fundamentally true, that we humans write stories and dramas because such activities reflect activity in which we are already engaged as creatures conscious that we have a past, a present, and a future. Such speculations, however, are beyond the theoretical scope of this book.

It is now appropriate to offer empirical confirmation for the perspective laid down in this and previous propositions in the present chapter. Along with my colleagues Joan Fee, Teresa Sullivan, and William McCready, I hypothesized that one could find patterns of religious images in respondents by simply asking them to describe how they felt about certain cosmic symbols—God, Jesus, Mary (the respondents were a sample of young adult Catholics), and Heaven (the exact wording of the questions can be found in the appendix). I was particularly interested in "warm" images, for I thought they would both reflect happy experiences in the family of origin and satisfying experiences in the family of procreation. A factor composed of images of Jesus as "warm," Mary as "warm," God as "lover," and Heaven as a paradise of pleasure and delight was constructed to test this hypothesis. Not only did such warm religious images relate to a happy childhood with the joyous parents, they also predicted sexual fulfillment and marital satisfaction, racial and social attitudes toward sexual permissiveness, alienation and commitment through the act of both the church and society and religious devotion. Those who were high on the "warm" images scale were more likely to be socially committed, politically active, and concerned about racial justice and less likely—despite their political and social liberalism—to approve of premarital sex and living together before marriage (perhaps, because their images of God as a lover imply public fidelity). All these correlations were statistically significant and some of them quite powerful (see *The Young Catholic Family*). They also correlated strongly with "ecstatic" experiences and experiences of "purpose" and experiences of the "sacred."

It need hardly be said that all four images are, in fact, relational marriages, implying a story of a warm or passionate relationship with cosmic personages. A warm family background relates to warm religious stories which relate to sexual fulfillment and a happy marriage, and also relate to social and political commitment and to rejection of sexual promiscuity. They are also affected by experiences of hope, joy, purpose, and awe. Indeed, doctrinal orthodoxies do not relate, for example, to frequency of prayer, for religious images do. One does not pray to an idea, one prays to a personage, if not to a Person. Similarly, formal education does not seem to affect religious imagery. But human relationships do. Images, in other words, seem to result from relationship and to be oriented to relationship and to be divorced from both instruction in ideas and convictions about ideas.

The correlations are not overwhelming. Religious stories can scarcely be expected to be the *only* fact relating to sexual fulfillment in marriage. The correlation between a joint husband and wife religious imagery scale and sexual fulfillment is .25—rising to .37 in the ninth and tenth year of marriage (since our sample involved young people under thirty we could not go beyond the ninth and tenth years of the marriage); as social science relationships go these are quite impressive, especially because they are linkages between aspects of human behavior which would never have been investigated if the present theory had not been elaborated and hypothetically predicted in such relationships. Religious images are important. The "stories of God" we carry in our preconscious powerfully affect our lives, even if they are—as turns out to be the case—totally unaffected by our formal, discursive religious education. As my student Thomas Hoffman has demonstrated, images of God also have a powerful effect on social and political commitment and involvement, although doctrinal orthodoxy does not. It is our stories of God, rather than our religious ideas, which lead to political and social commitment.

The creative imagination, then, can produce more or less warm, hopeful, and encouraging stories. This observation leads us to our next proposition.

3.6 *There is an enormous variety in the religious stories that human persons create for themselves. A person's story is shaped by biological, cultural, educational, psychological, ethnic, and biographic factors.*

Even within given religious heritages much can be made of particular religious symbols. Thus, young Catholic Christians have available as resources to resonate, represent, and rearticulate their grace experiences in the images of God and Jesus and Mary and Heaven. But, in their exercise of the art of story telling and song singing to themselves they may produce many different combinations as they play the game of cosmic bricollage. Our research emphasizes the familial determinants of variety—relationships with parents, between parents, and relationships with spouse. Other research, doubtless, could uncover other background factors. The point is that the representation of the experience of grace and the articulation of hopefulness—probably the grace/hope experience itself—are profoundly affected not only by the repertory of symbols we bring to such experiences from the religious heritage into which we have been born (more of that in a subsequent chapter), but also by our own personal life, background, and social experiences.

Some springs may be more renewing for me than others not because the spring weather is different (though in middle western America that is certainly a possibility), but because I am at least partially a different person this spring than I was last spring. Similarly on some given gray and rainy days I may not even notice the beautiful woman I pass on the street (for which God forgive me!). There are unquestionably other persons who will be more moved by both these phenomena than I am, and, doubtless, yet others who will be less moved. Perhaps some pathetic creatures cannot be moved at all, and there will be others whose ideological, intellectual convictions demand that they must resist the hope implications of their grace experiences.

Stories are similar in that they tend to be made up of similar components. They are different in that we all tell different stories.

I wish to emphasize once again that we are not yet dealing with formal religion (though we have spoken of religious heritages necessarily because these heritages affect the repertory of potential symbols with which we come to our experiences of grace). I am still talking about raw experiences unrelated to church, doctrine, creed, even to explicit reflection about the nature of "whatever" is experienced as renewing. Nor am I suggesting that experiences of grace are the "origin" of religion in a given person. Much of what is "religious" in us comes from our denominations, our creeds, our catechisms, and may even exist in conflict with our personal experiences of grace. I am merely asserting that if it were not for our capacity to experience grace, religion would not exist and that the power of religion comes from its "origins" in the creative imagination where grace is experienced. The fact that religious images correlate far more powerfully with human behavior than formal religious education confirms the utility of this perspective.

Religion, of course, becomes reflective, ecclesiastical, propositional, and creedal. But, in its "origins" it is as commonplace, as secular as everyday as the smell of the southwest wind or the attractive body of another human being—in so far as the warm wind and the gracious body occasionally seem to tell a story of renewal and of hope, or, more precisely, produce experiences in us which lead us to tell such stories.

3.7 *The primary purpose of religious stories is the articulation of the relationship between good and evil. There are four scenarios: optimism, pessimism, fatalism, and hope.*

The theoretical origins of this proposition are based on the work of Paul Ricoeur on the symbolism of evil. Briefly, there would be no need for an experience of grace if there were no evil in our lives, for then we would clearly lead an existence not of promise, but of fulfillment. It is precisely the "ungood" that is mixed with good that drives us to tell stories.

According to Ricoeur, there have been four fundamental responses to the ultimate questions of good and evil—the optimistic (which Ricoeur sees in Egyptian religion); the pessimistic (as represented by Mesopotamian religious symbols); the fatalistic (to be found in post-Homeric Greece); and the hopeful (as manifest by the Israelites' religion).

The optimistic world view sees reality as ultimately good, though tinged with some sadness and evil which are not of major moment. The pessimistic view sees the world as a cruel, hostile, and unsympathetic place. The fatalistic perspective shares the same grim view, but, unlike the pessimistic, sees little point in attempting to deal with or manipulate the hostile powers which dominate the cosmos. Finally, the hopeful perspective does not deny the cosmic battle, but believes in the precarious triumph of good; in this perspective, death, evil, and suffering have much to say, but they do not completely possess the last word.

It is obviously a long way from Ricoeur's typology to a survey questionnaire, but we responded that there might be six major ultimate value responses among modern Americans. The optimistic thrust, we speculated, might be divided into an uncomplicated religious optimism and an equally uncomplicated nonreligious or secular optimism. (We do not use uncomplicated in a pejorative sense, but rather to indicate that the belief system tends to minimize the problem of evil.) The pessimistic approach might be either fatalistic and resigned (like the Stoics) or angry. Between optimism and pessimism, we hypothesized a neutral stance in which the person expressed gratitude for past benefits. The hopeful approach, much as in the past, would tip the scales ever so slightly to favor of good in the cosmic war in heaven. Thus, the six possible interpretative responses to life problems would look something like this:

1. Religious optimism: "God will take care of everything, so there is no need to worry."
2. Secular optimism: "Everything will turn out for the best somehow."
3. Grateful acceptance: "We must be thankful for the good things that have happened to us despite the bad that we have to endure."
4. Anger: "It is unfair and unjust that we should have to suffer."
5. Resignation: "There is nothing that can be done; what will be will be."
6. Hopefulness: "There is no denying the evil of what is happening, but the last word has not been said yet."

McCready develops five vignettes dealing with terminal illness, being drafted into military, a parent's death, the birth of a retarded child, and a natural disaster and querried respondents first by open-ended questions and then by pre-coded questions based on the open-ended pretest. On the responses that they chose to each of these vignettes, four religious types emerged: The religious optimist, the hopeful, the secular optimist, and the pessimist. In subsequent analysis he discovered that income, education, religious background, region of the country, relationships with parents and friends, and marital satisfaction all correlate with the basic belief typology. I also discovered in my own research that there was a powerful correlation between hopefulness (in the narrow sense in which we use the term in this research) and intense religious experiences. It also developed that such basic orientations affected such things as racial attitudes, authoritarian or anti-authoritarian dispositions, and attitudes toward the role of women, which in all cases the "hopeful" respondents (again in the narrow sense in which this word was used in this research) tended to be less authoritarian and more "liberal" than the optimists, with the pessimists being rather like the hopeful. Thus, one's reactions to incidents of suffering and injustice and tragedy can be put together in a meaningful pattern. These patterns do respond to Ricoeur's paradigm of the reaction to evil, and they do correlate both with background variables and present attitudes and activities. Finally, in our subsequent research on young Catholic adults we also discovered that there was a relationship between images of warmth and responses of hopefulness.

The "basic belief" research was done before we were able to develop our methodology of getting directly at religious images, and represents philosophical or ethical derivations from religious experience (reflections on stories of God) rather than a direct measure of such experiences and images themselves. The ultimate value typology deals with the in-

The Frequency Distribution of the Ultimate Value Types

Ultimate Value Type	Frequency	Percentage
Religious optimist	320	22
Hopeful	326	22
Secular optimist	210	14
Pessimist	344	24
Diffuse	257	18
Missing data	10	—
TOTAL	1,467	100

tellect rather than the creative imagination, though the intellect can be expected to reflect to some considerable extent what goes on in the creative imagination.

It also seemed to us—though the point may not be especially pertinent for this book—that there may be a distinction between religious ethics and philosophical ethics. If the experience of grace is action oriented, producing action first, then reflection, then it carries an ethical dynamic of its own, perhaps different from and certainly more powerful than philosophical ethics which may or may not be derived from such experiences. When I arise from my dune reinvigorated by the advent of spring and plunge enthusiastically back into my work, I am, it seems, acting on a raw and primal ethical imperative which says, in effect, "Celebrate life." I may also have philosophical reasons for going back to work (to say nothing of the economic reasons which come from the obligation to meet report deadlines). But the ethics of the creative imagination, I would suggest, are far more powerful than the ethics of the intellect (which is not to say that they ought not be subject to careful review and examination by the intellect, or that the elaboration of formal reflective philosophical systems is inappropriate or unnecessary).

Similarly, when I smile at the woman on the street I respond to the raw creative imperative, "respond gracefully to grace," an imperative which will have enormous impact on any future relationship I may have with her, or, indeed, on whether there will be any future relationship at all. Obviously my future relationship with her or with any woman must be guided by ethical values solidly grounded in reason and articulated in clear moral propositions. Yet, is it too much to suggest that these propositions derive at least some of their binding power from the raw respect and admiration which accompany my renewal of hope? When hope is articulated even so simply as in "respond gracefully to grace" it has already moved a step beyond my experience toward reflection?

At the risk of repeating a previous theme, I am not, heaven save us, advocating an irrational religion or an irrational ethic. I am suggesting something much more modest: much of the powerful dynamic of religious and ethical behavior comes from stories and experiences which spring up spontaneously in the creative imagination as our response to experiences of grace and which are not irrational or superrational, but simply prerational, requiring subsequent reflection, indeed, but not likely to be replaced in their power or importance by subsequent reflection.

Fatalism and pessimism are not merely philosophical systems but also stories that individuals have told for the purpose of validating their own lives. They seem almost to be negations of grace. The problem of "negative" experiences needs to be examined more carefully. In negative mystical experiences (experiences in which the "other" is perceived rather like Bergmann's spider-god) there are family background conditions such as the absence of religious belief and the lack of affection which seem to create a predisposition for negative experiences of the ultimate. Our attempt to sort out the American population on Ricoeur's dimensions did not uncover very many pessimists or fatalists: persons whose experiences incline them here to reject experiences of grace or to put rather different interpretations on them or, perhaps, to rearticulate and represent their experiences in different stories or different belief systems derived from the stories. The existence of fatalists and pessimists does not invalidate our theoretical perspective because in the beginning I claimed no universality for my theoretical positions, only propensities and tendencies. The fatalists and the pessimists are more of a problem, I think, for Professor Lionel Tiger than they are for me, though he would contend, I suspect, that given a chance to analyze the world view of the pessimists and the fatalists he would find more than a few traces of hope. But if the fatalists and the pessimists are not a challenge to religious theory, they are a challenge to research on religion.

3.8 *There is no evidence that the proportions who have high capacity for grace experiences and a high need to represent those experiences in "stories of grace" have undergone any substantial change in the course of human history.*

Clifford Geertz once jokingly remarked that some day he would do a book called "Belief and Unbelief Among Primitive Peoples" and would subtitle it "A Study of Faith and Hypocrisy." Not all primitives in the contemporary world are devout. Presumably, not all members of our ancestral primitive groups were devout either, and not all moderns are undevout. Neither education nor age nor youthfulness affect warm religious images or hopeful or optimistic world views. There may well be changing patterns of ecclesiastical and formal religious behavior as the structures of human society and the convictions of human culture change. But there is no evidence that the need for hope or the experience of grace or the articulation of grace experiences in stories has changed at all in the human condition. One-third of the American population report intense ecstatic experiences, four-fifths report some kind of experience of grace, and approximately the same number respond hopefully or optimistically to the problems of evil in the human condition; one can hardly assume a drift away from religion as I have used the term religion so far in this theoretical presentation.

Religion, according to the theory presented in this study, "originates" in our experiences of hope, experiences which are articulated and resonated in symbols which are stories. These stories link the past, the present, and the future of our lives to some overarching story that gives meaning not only to our existence, but also to the existence of the universe. These stories tend to direct the future of our lives, correlating with social, political, and relational behavior. Precisely because they account for our past and our present, they also provide a trajectory for our future.

Chapter Four
The Other

In the raw experiences of grace, the idea of "God" as such does not arise. If a person uses an image of "God" in his immediate articulation and resonance to his/her experience of grace, then the reason very likely is that the person already had the God symbol in his repertory of symbol components. The "God" symbol is secondary in the creative imagination to such symbols as fire, water, spring, birth, sex. God is an abstract image, indeed, a picture that is something less than a portrait while the other images are concrete and vivid.

4.1 *That which is encountered in the experience of grace is perceived as "other."*

"Other" (or "otherness") becomes "The Other" upon reflection, though the reflection usually is immediate. One encounters "something" in renewing grace experiences, something related to the spring dew or the lovely woman, but in some fashion also unrelated, intruding itself into my life, or is perceived intruding itself into my life and renewing me. While I am aware that whatever it is, is not like me, it also seems in some ways to be like me and so I attempt to personify it, though personification does not reduce the wonder, but enhances it. (Hence, the argument about a "personal" God is mostly irrelevant. When we bestow personhood on whatever it is we encounter, we do it honor the only way we can.) Perhaps, the reason "other" becomes "The Other" is that grace reveals to us "The Gracious"; whenever we have encountered graciousness in our lives it has been loving. That which has been encountered in the grace experience—fascinating, terrifying, mystifying, hilarious, apparently loving—seems not only to be "other" and "The Other," but "Another," "Another" which would not be offended, on the contrary would be flattered if we referred to it as a "Thou."

We encounter otherness in everything and, hence, we are at times animists. We encounter it especially in some things—mountains, lakes, storms, rivers, reproductions—and, hence, we are at times polytheists. At other times otherness seems to be a unity implicit in all the diversity of our experience, and, hence, we tend to be monotheists. Sometimes the other that is experienced seems (almost) totally bound to the reality through which we experience it, and, hence, we are immanentists. And sometimes it seems almost totally withdrawn from that reality with perhaps only the tip of its fingernails (should it have fingernails, which seems unlikely) linked to the reality through which we have encountered it, and, hence, we are transcendentalists.

Each individual person is capable at various times and under various circumstances of resonating to otherness in one of the ways which has been historically identified with religion; thus animism, polytheism, monotheism, transcendentalism, rather than constituting an evolutionary process are differences of resonance within the human personality (it is possible—though hardly documentable—that the proportions of the human race which respond one way or the other have changed through the course of human history).

4.2 *Otherness is undifferentiated and yet complex. Its initial impact on the creative imagination is plastic and fluid; hence, the multiplicity of the symbolizations of otherness.*

Since this book is not concerned with discussion about whether "The Other" really is, but only about our perception of it (him/her, whatever), the issue presently is not whether "The Other" is, in fact, both undifferentiated and complex, but whether the impact of otherness in our raw experience of grace is that of a reality both undifferentiated and complex, undifferentiated in its renewing power, but extraordinarily complex in the manifestations of its renewing power and in the impact of those manifestations on our personality and behavior. Since the first impact of otherness on our personality is on the creative imagination which is endlessly fluid, shifting, dynamic, it is inevitable that we should perceive otherness as both simple and undifferentiated on the one hand and variegated and complex on the other. Images of otherness and symbolization of the Other vary enormously in the human condition precisely because there is such a vast range of possible experiences and of humans who experience.

That stories of God do vary enormously is obvious from the study of the history of religions. Content analysis of descriptions of grace experiences would validate both this and the previous proposition.

In our research on Catholic young adults, my colleagues and I developed a series of four questions designed to measure in a preliminary sort of way the content of the religious imagination. The four questions dealing with God, Jesus, Mary, and Heaven are presented in an appendix. Each question is in effect a matrix, and the respondent's answer to each question traces a line through the matrix. These four lines, we contend, constitute a preliminary and very rough map of the religious imagination. Factor analysis discovered two dimensions in both the Jesus and Mary questions, a "warm" and a "cold" dimension, two in the God question, one representing God as mother and lover, and the other floating on the remaining items in the question. Three factors could be found in the responses to the Heaven question, one stressing Heaven as a place of union and peace, another Heaven as a shadowy place and a spiritual place, and a third, imagining Heaven as a life of action, as a life better than the present life and a paradise of pleasure and delight. In addition four items, Jesus as warm, Mary as warm, Heaven as a paradise of pleasure and delight, and God as a lover, seem to cut meaningfully across the four questions. It is our contention that these seven factors and one scale can all be considered for operational purposes "stories" of God. My colleagues and I have demonstrated in *The Young Catholic Family* and *The Young Catholic Adult* the very considerable predictive power of these stories. Continued reference will be made to them in this book. The reader interested in technical documentation should, however, consult the pertinent research monograph.

4.3 *The symbolization of a grace experience is the result of both the experience itself and of the background of the experiencing person (or group).*

What we make of otherness, whether and how we translate it into "The Other" and whether and how "The Other" more formally becomes "God" result from a blend of the experience of grace itself and the background which the experiencing person brings to his encounter with grace. I have thus far been able to avoid the issue of whether one needs an explicit "referent" or a symbol to be religious. I would define as "religious" any symbol which deals with an experience of otherness, whether that otherness be perceived as beyond the confines of this world or not. Otherness does not have to become "The Other," much less God, for the experience and the symbol to be religious. It need merely be *wonderful*, that is to say, stirring up *wonder*. Furthermore, since the experience of "otherness" is an experience so fluid and plastic, it is quite possible for it to be experienced as and resonated to as something almost totally imminent in this world. As long as that which is experienced is perceived as distinct from the ordinary and as containing, however vaguely, meaning and purpose, then it is or at least can be in some way "wonderful" and "gracious." Many Marxists, for example, have a tendency to view Marx and his writings as at least quasi-wonderful and thus participating in "otherness." For them the prophet and his writings are, indeed, an experience of grace, a revalidation of hope, a promise for a future, a story partially told and yet waiting to be told, a story with which their own story can be linked.

"Otherness" is not necessarily perceived as the "totally other," though it often is and there is, perhaps, a tendency for that which is simply "other" (including, for example, Marx and his writing) to become so important, so distinctive from everything else that for all practical purposes it becomes "totally other."

There are, then, so many different images of God because there are so many different experiences of grace and so many different backgrounds which are brought to these experiences. If we tell different "stories of God," the reason is that we come to our encounters with grace with different stories already partially told and have different experiences of grace.

On one level of evidence this proposition can be confirmed merely by considering the various "stories of God" presented in the different religions of humans, an incredible variety of stories (though, perhaps, with a common underlying theme which need not concern us here). At another level this proposition is also confirmed by the evidence gathered in a National Opinion Research Center (NORC) project showing that family background experiences as well as experiences in the present family, previous religious orientation, education, region of the country, and other background variables affect both one's image of God and one's reaction to life's tragedies. If we had had a loving father and mother, we are considerably more likely to have loving images of God and loving relationships with our spouse. In other words, the image of God as loving intervenes between loving experiences with parents and loving experiences with spouses. The image encodes and keeps alive the memory of the former and predisposes for the encounter with the latter. A picture of a loving God links love in the family of origin with love in the family of procreation.

Furthermore, our story of God affects our social and political commitment precisely because it relates to antecedent family experiences. The religious images that my colleagues and I have measured seem to encode experiences in the family of origin and link them to experiences in later life both in the intimacy of the family and in relationships with the larger society.

Finally, it must be insisted that otherness (or the wonderful) is encountered as such in an interlude in which the whole personality is involved but without self-conscious reflection. Afterwards, one may ask whether that which was encountered was "sacred," but this is a reflective question, an attempt to impose upon or draw from the experience a philosophical or sociological category of analysis.

4.4 *The available repertory of symbols and past symbolization affects not only the symbolization of our present experiences, but the nature of that experience itself.*

The wonderful that I experience today, in addition to being shaped by all my other background experiences, is also powerfully shaped by the religious symbols and religious stories I have available and by my previous experiences of grace. Those with warm or passionate "stories of God" are more likely to perceive otherness as warm and passionate in their current experiences of grace than those who lack such stories.

The NORC evidence, which showed a correlation between the experiences of grace and the images of God, documents partially the truth of this proposition, though it is impossible without longitudinal research following the same respondents for many years to sort out whether the experience or the story is prior.

4.5 *"Belief in God" can exist without hopeful experiences and such experiences can occur for those who do not "believe in God," and need not result in "belief in God."*

Whence comes "God?" In the context of this theory, "God" is the image created to articulate and resonate the conviction that the otherness encountered in experiences of grace is Another and even The Other. That which renews us and reinforces our hopes seems to be both knowing and loving, and, therefore, we "personify" it and even anthropomorphize it because there is no other way to speak of such knowing and loving otherness. (Incidentally, might it not be appropriate to call for a moratorium on patronizing the anthropomorphic language of less "educated" peoples? How can you talk about otherness save through anthropomorphic terms? Paul Tillich's "Totally Other," for example, may be superior as a concept to that of the Irish Catholic's "great monsignor in the sky," but both are anthropomorphic. Monsignors are capable occasionally of knowing and loving. It is not altogether clear that Tillich's "Totally Other" would be at all interested in such activities, particularly with such lowly beings as us.).

The image of God comes much earlier, however, in the religious process than the rational-philosophical question of "belief in God." If the image of God is not as utterly spontaneous in our creative imaginations as in the image of sunlight or moonlight or springtime, it is, nonetheless, almost universally available to humankind. The Encyclopedist may well have been right when he said that man (his word) creates

God to his own image and likeness, though it is, perhaps, more appropriate to say that humankind creates its image of God in response to its experience of otherness. Our "pictures" of The Other are acts of the creative imagination and are substantially anterior to the philosophical and catechetical and creedal question of whether we "believe in God." There are, it would seem, many persons who reject belief in God, and yet who have encountered otherness and are, indeed, renewed in their hope and lead lives of hopefulness. Nor does one have to document the fact that there are not a few people in the world who profess creedal belief in God whose images of God are anything but Wonderful. There are then those who experience and believe in the Wonderful but reject the philosophical concept of God, and there are those who adhere to the philosophical concept of God but do not invest it with any images from experiences of the Wonderful. Grace can be experienced without God and God can be believed in without grace being experienced.

4.6 *Some persons, places, times, and behaviors are thought of as especially likely to reveal otherness (The Wonderful) because the images of them seem to be especially suitable for articulating, replicating, representing, and resonating our experiences of otherness.*

Some objects because of their shape (such as a tree linking earth and heaven) or their purpose (the body of a member of the opposite sex) or their importance (food and drink) and some times—ends and beginnings, equinoxes, solstices—are "special." They are places and events which readily predispose us to hope or especially challenge that hope. They represent situations in which The Other is somewhat more likely to be encountered, where otherness is more likely to intrude, where God is especially likely to reveal himself (sometimes in potentially terrifying ways, so terrifying that some sacred times and places are to be avoided—hence, "tabooed"). We tend to be ambivalent about such loci and tempora of otherness precisely because otherness is both fascinating and frightening. While we welcome the hopefulness that comes in our experience of grace, we may easily be terrified by the demands hopefulness makes and by the apparent *awesomeness* of whatever is making the demands.

The person who discovers a sacred time or place need not know it is sacred until he has reflected on his experience of wonder in it. There are other places (St. Peter's Basilica in Rome for me being one) which are monumentally "sacred" but in which The Other or otherness seems to be totally absent (I do not say that God is not in St. Peter's, but merely that I do not find her/him there).

That sacred times and places abound in human society is hardly a proposition that requires proof, though useful empirical research could be done on the process by which individuals or small communities create their own times and places of "otherness" and on the impact of such "wonderful" times and places on their lives.

Times and places of otherness are "sacraments" in the sense that they represent situations and circumstances in which "otherness" reveals itself. For the purpose of this theory it is not necessary to hypothesize about the outer limits of potential sacramentality. One may be content with saying that some times and places seem more likely to play a "sacramental" role than others. However, religious thinkers like Karl Rahmer, David Tracy, and Nathan Scott insist on philosophical grounds that the potential of revelation must be in all beings in order that some beings might have special potential. Everything must be a sacrament, in other words, before some things can become Sacraments. Sociologists more modestly will be content with saying that a large number of things seem capable of triggering experiences of grace and then in their residual images representing and articulating that experience.

Intense religious experiences have been triggered according to research McCready and I have done by the following events in the order of frequency in which they are mentioned:

Listening to music
Prayer
Beauties of nature such as sunset
Moments of quiet reflection
Attending church service
Listening to a sermon
Watching little children
Reading the Bible
Being alone in church
Reading a poem or a novel
Childbirth
Sexual lovemaking
One's own creative work
Looking at a painting
Physical exercise

Most people come to their experiences of grace shaped by rational if not by philosophical concepts of God which they have derived from their religious heritage. Such concepts influence both the experience of grace itself and the representation of that experience in a story of grace. Chronologically, the concept may come before the experience. But the concept is not capable of capturing or constraining or defining the experience; often the experience explodes beyond the concept or has an impact totally at odds with the concept. Concepts are religious only derivatively, that is, they represent reflection on raw and primal experiences which impact on and explode in the creative imagination. Religious concepts have far less impact on our lives than do the stories of God or the stories of grace which well up out of our creative imaginations—and at some time are at variance with our religious concepts. Though concepts may chronologically precede experiences of grace, they are psychologically derivative from them, and utterly dependent for their dynamic vitality on them. It is far more important to know what a person's "story of otherness" is than to know whether he "believes in God."

Chapter Five

Vertical Community

God and church were postponed from consideration in the early chapters of this book, not because they are unimportant religiously, but because if we focus on them prematurely in our investigation of religion, we may overlook the raw materials of religion from which both our concepts of God and our ecclesiastical structures are drawn and on which both concept and structure depend for strength and vitality.

In this chapter we will look at the church not as an institution or even as an existing community, but rather as a heritage, a traditional arrangement of symbols which has been passed down through the years by groups of human beings who have associated themselves with these symbol arrangements. Most children learn about God before coming into contact with their church, and many if not most learn about "graciousness" before they have any formal concept of God (a point to which we will return in a subsequent chapter on the family). Religious heritages, then, are anterior to, wider than, and more powerful as socializing agents than formal denominational structures.

Though the propositions in this chapter are almost entirely derived from existing philosophical and literary writing on symbol and metaphor, some social science empirical validation is to be found in the research that McCready and I have done on ultimate values and religious imagery. All of the propositions are technically falsifiable or verifiable by empirical research. Whether such research would be profitable might be questionable.*

5.1 *Religious heritages are systems (or arrangements) of symbols (or stories) designed to articulate a previous intense experience.*

Symbols (religious or not) are dense, polyvalent, and multifaceted. Stories say many different things at the same time. Symbols/stories emit, therefore, many different cues. The arrangement of symbols into "systems" involves not merely the interlinking of symbolic raw material—pulling together of stories around a more basic story—but precisely in the interlinking process the stressing of specific and consistent cues running through the various connected symbols/stories.

Let us take, for example, stories of freedom, rebirth, reunion, renewal; stories might be told as tales of springs following winters, of liberators overthrowing oppressors, of friends being reunited, and of love beginning again. In stories of spring, liberation, and reconciliation there are many different cues, not all of which can be emphasized. A given story of spring, for example, may omit the emphasis on the inevitable return of winter. A story of liberation may ignore the fact that the enemy still lurks out in the wilderness. A story of the reunion of friends may choose to stress the dan-

---

* As we shall see in subsequent chapters, McCready's research does demonstrate the power of the family as a religious socialization institution, and the transmission of "ultimate values" such as hopefulness or pessimism from parent to children. We do not yet have available data to test whether religious imagery is also transmitted from parent to children, though we do know there is a connection between family "joyousness" and religious images; also, that husbands and wives influence each others' religious imagery. See, especially Chapter 10 for reference to the discussion by William and Nancy McCready of early religious socialization and sexual identity as creating a predisposing context for later experiences of grace.

gers which threaten the continuation of friendship. A story of renewed love may ironically observe that before the day is over the lovers will be quarreling again. On the level of the creative imagination no emphasis is better or worse than another. If one chooses to arrange a collection of such stories into some sort of coherent system, one will do so precisely by emphasizing the consistent cues in each of the stories. Thus, in the Christian spring story the emphasis is on definitive liberation, definitive rebirth, unshatterable reconciliation, and permanent love. Such an arrangement of symbols may or may not depict the reality in which we find ourselves. But the coherent arrangement of stories is precisely what constitutes the basis for an inheritance or a tradition. The central or "privileged" story of the death and resurrection of Jesus connotes implacable victory. The other related stories—liberation and communion echoing the Jewish passover story and the renewal of covenant echoing the Sinai story—are all linked with and in a certain sense subjected to the dominant spring "rebirth" or "resurrection" theme of the principal story.

Note that this arrangement of symbols exists in the preconscious before it gets articulated as a formal "belief system" or faith. It existed in the preconscious of the early Christians as their attitudes and behavior are disclosed to us—through whatever overlays of theological reflection—in the New Testament. It probably also exists (though this is subject to empirical research) in the preconscious of many contemporary Christians before the acquisition of and to some extent independently of formal faith propositions.

Thus, our research on the survival of the Madonna image among Americans indicates that two-thirds of American Catholics say that they are extremely likely to think of the Madonna as "warm" and "gentle" and "comforting" and "patient," as are two-fifths of the non-Catholic spouses married to Catholics in our sample (more than half of the Methodists

85

and Baptists and 37 percent of those who have no religion at all). For both Catholics and Protestants the Mary symbol encodes a childhood experience of a mother who was warm, affectionate, devout, but also deeply involved in the family decision-making processes, an androgenous mother related to a Madonna symbol which, in turn, relates to sexual fulfillment in marriage both for men and women. Mary, in other words, tells a story of God which resonates with and recaptures the experience achieved through maternity (the experience of being mothered) in childhood, and makes maternity or shared maternity fruitful and pleasurable in adult life.

The arrangement of symbols in the creative imagination is not logical, but poetic. It is an exercise in bricollage in which stories are playfully jammed together without any regard for how they might make logical sense. The later imposition of logical constraint and restraint on the playful and often manic inventiveness of the creative imagination is an inevitable and necessary activity. However, logical and rational minds will find enormously disturbing the apparent contradiction of the poetic imagination. (Is Jesus Adam or Moses or Abraham, or a prophet, or a king? Those who had the initial experience seemed freely to have used all terms to describe him without any care about being precise as to in what sense he reflected the work of these predecessors. The logical mind is disturbed by their lack of precision.)

It is necessary in our era to separate the stories, to sort out the components, to systematize them logically and to subject them to philosophical critique and elaboration. Yet, much of the elemental power and attraction of the story is lost in this process of logical and coherent elaboration (think, for example, of what professors of English literature can do with the plays of Shakespeare). The resulting logical, philosophical, theological and catechetic systems are useful and necessary. But, unless it is possible to return from them to the original stories (with what Paul Ricoeur calls, "the second naiveté") such imposing systems may enjoy very little vitality.

5.2 *Religious heritages are transmitted primarily by the use of symbol systems to replicate the experiences which gave rise to them.*

For most of human history the telling of stories and the singing of songs, the celebration of feasts and the dancing of dances were the only forms of religious socialization. It was not necessary to make the pilgrimage from the first to the second naiveté. People could live with the first naiveté. (Which does not mean, however, that there were not some folks who did unpack and then reassemble the stories. There may be a higher proportion of full professors in the modern world, but that does not mean that there were necessarily less critical minds in earlier ages. More likely there was simply less time for those with the critical minds to engage in unpacking symbols.)

The telling of tales and the singing of songs, the dancing of dances, the celebrating of feasts were not intended to provide propositional knowledge. They were intended, rather, to re-create experiences, to reach into the preconscious or the creative imagination and call forth past experiences and link these experiences—poetically, not logically or philosophically—to the basic symbol arrangement which constitutes the heritage.

Thus, to take a festival which is far more reflective and propositional than most, the Jewish Seder, eating the passover together is much more oriented toward the re-creation of past experience than it is toward giving ethical or ritual instruction. Midnight Mass at Christmas, one of the most powerful festivals in the Catholic Christian tradition, is designed to re-create the experience of light and darkness with which the early Church thought of Bethlehem more than it is to propound a certain catechetical or theological proposition about the Incarnation. Both Seder and Midnight Mass do not seek to impose stories on those who participate, but, rather, to stir up experiences of light, dark, of fidelity and infidelity, unity and disunity, of warmth and cold, experiences which the participants have had themselves in the course of their lives, and link these experiences through the dominating stories of the religious heritage.

Easter and Passover (in most languages the feasts have the same name) are fascinating because they represent layer upon layer of religious experience, the unleavened bread representing the pre-Sinai spring festival of an agricultural people, the paschal lamb representing the pre-Sinai experience of a pastoral people, the fire and the water representing the male and female elements in the Christian liturgy of Holy Saturday (in which the fire of the candle is plunged into the water), clearly following the pagan spring fertility rite. (The fiery cloud and the water of the Red Sea are a somewhat more obscure Israelite allusion to such pagan symbolism.) Thus, one has fire, water, paschal lamb, and unleavened bread as pagan pictures to which has been added the Jewish symbolisms of people, liberation, and new life over which has been added a Christian interpretation which does not so much change, but deepen the meaning of peoplehood, liberation, and new life. All three symbols are used precisely to stir up spring images of life beginning again for a new people, a new humanity. Such symbols reach deep into the past, and deep into the human preconscious and unconscious.

When I propose this description of heritage transmission to Catholic educators they are frequently upset for fear that religious "truth" will be lost in the process as though the fire and the water, the Easter vigil, or the crib scene can ever really be misunderstood. What such educators do not seem to realize is that most religious socialization through the course of human history has occurred precisely through such techniques, unself-consciously used. As formal classroom indoctrination in creedal and catechetical propositions is relatively recent and still relatively limited, the NORC research on Catholic education shows that while the schools are important, particularly in integrating young people closer into the Catholic community, the family is by far the more powerful religious educator. Family religious socialization is more likely to be the socializer of story and festival, of Christmas and the baby Jesus and of "God's mommy" (a concept which does not bother the children because from their point of view if God is anyone worth knowing he has got to have a mommy).

Mexican-American Catholicism is still primarily transmitted through the experience of festival and story. In any conflict with the propositional religion which middle-class Mexican-American children acquire in the Catholic schools and the pictures or stories of religion which they acquire in their home, the latter is easily more powerful.

Catholic adolescents (as opposed to Catholic young adults) seem to have acquired, apparently through their mothers and apparently as a result of the Second Vatican Council, a very different story of God in which the emphasis on God as mother and lover is more strongly perceived. Indeed, Catholic teen-agers are twice as likely as Catholic young adults to have a high score on a scale which emphasizes God as the lover and mother and Heaven as an active better life than as a paradise of pleasure and delight. This change in religious consciousness has occurred without any modification of doctrinal teaching. But it is the result of a new religious context in the relationship between children and young mothers who were profoundly influenced by the Vatican Council (perhaps, because of among other things the Council created a climate—despite the wishes of church leaders—for young mothers to be able to freely rethink their attitudes toward birth control and sex).

5.3 *Symbol systems or story arrangements are passed on within a religious tradition especially through the preconscious in early childhood. There is no guarantee, however, that such transmission will necessarily be consistent with the overarching emphasis of the Great Tradition.*

Some families or some groups, perhaps even some denominations within a religious heritage, may rearrange the stories in such a way that, while they are technically within the doctrinal boundaries of the heritage, they may become a collection of stories, dances, songs, festivals, at greater or lesser variance from the "privileged" story. Parents could easily (and often do) draw from the Christmas story the conclusion that Jesus was a good little boy to his mommy and daddy, not a bad little boy like you are (conveniently forgetting the incident of the twelve-year-old hiding in the temple). If this should become the overriding story pattern that a child acquires, he is likely to think of Jesus as an unattractive and forbidding person. Our evidence shows that young people who grew up in an environment where the father's religion is not joyous are more likely to think of God as a judge and less likely precisely because of that different "story of God" to be committed to social justice and racial integration.

Similarly, families or even denominations may so rearrange the stories of the New Testament that the emphasis becomes not on God's liberating love, but on his punishing wrath. It may be possible to clothe such stories in doctrinal propositions which keep them within the bounds of theological orthodoxy. Yet, such stories are hardly compatible with what appears to be the central or privileged story of implacable, death-defying love, which is the privileged story of the Christian heritage.

Thus, it is perfectly possible for a person to be doctrinally orthodox, catechetically precise, and ritually devout and still possess preconscious religious dynamisms which are different from the dynamisms that the stories were designed to excite—especially when religious stories get involved with negative, emotional, and psychological sanctions.

It is necessary, therefore, to know not merely a person's propositional religion, but also his religious story. In our study of young Catholics, while there was no correlation between religious education and warm religious images (images which reflect most adequately the central Christian story), there was a relationship between warm religious images on the one hand and social and racial justice on the other hand. The point is *not* that propositional religion and story religion need be at odds with one another, but merely that they may be, and when they are, the fault usually lies in a defect in socialization of the religious imagination.

5.4 *Within any religious heritage there is a wide variety of cues from specific symbols and linkages among cues which are not inconsistent with the founding experience.*

5.5 *The arrangement and rearrangement of symbols within the heritage is also an exercise of the poetic capacity of the person and the group.*

5.6 *Rearrangement of cues and cue linkages occurs in response to new stimuli from the external environment and as a result of additional experiences of goodness.*

These three propositions are presented as a paradigm for the development not of doctrine, but symbol arrangement within a religious heritage. While rearrangements of symbols may occur which are at variance with the privileged story of a religious tradition, there are also other rearrangements which are consistent with the privileged story and merely reflect a somewhat different aspect of it appropriate for a different set of circumstances. An investigation of the religious history of any heritage will demonstrate that the cue linkages and the cues being linked are undergoing constant mutation. Thus, in many of the New Testament books one observes story dynamics that emphasize the return of Jesus to fulfill the promise of the principal story—God's implacable love for humans. One can find if one reenters the heritage, say in the fourteenth century, in a time of plague and destruction, the grim imagery of the "Dies Irae," and one sees in the modern era the arrangement of linkages and focus on human intimacy as a continuation and fulfillment of the promise of God's intimacy with his people.

It is beyond the scope of the present book to examine the historical and psychological factors involved in such symbol rearrangement, though new experiences of goodness which deepen and enrich the heritage are normally a response to the changing challenges that come from the human environment to which the individual or the group belong. The rediscovery of marital intimacy as revelatory may be thought of as a Christian response to the much stronger emphasis on marital fulfillment in our era (an emphasis which may come from the fact that marriages last four times as long as they did a century and a half ago).

Husbands' and wives' stories of God tend to converge particularly after the first five years of marriage and particularly when the marriages are sexually fulfilling. It is as though by the lives they live and by their sexual relations husbands and wives are telling each other a "story of God," which, in satisfying marriages anyway, become similar with the passage of time. The flow of influence seems to be especially from husband to wife. For the first years of the marriage wives whose husbands think of God as a mother and a lover and Heaven as an action-filled life of pleasure and delight are no different from wives whose husbands do not have such stories of God in their own religious stories. However, in the second five years of marriage the wives with husbands who have benign stories of God and of Heaven who also have such stories doubles (from 25 percent to almost 50 percent), whereas wives whose husbands do not have such benign stories fall from 21 percent to 10 percent in their proportion having such benign images of God and Heaven.

Religious experiences differ in part at different eras in history (and in different persons and groups at the same time in history) as so, too, do the arrangements of religious stories to convey the full impact of one's experience of grace. While the Catholic Church's propositional teaching of the indissolubility of marriage may remain immutable (though canonical practices for determining what is a sacramental marriage are not completely beyond change), the experience of marital intimacy as an occasion for a story of grace is different than it was in an era when marriages lasted on an average twelve years and when humans were not equipped with the values and vocabulary of Freudian psychology with which to reflect upon their intimacy.

The creative imagination cannot be kept in a straightjacket. Within the paradigm of the privileged story of a tradition, wide varieties of "plots" can and will develop.

5.7 *In a complex society all major religious heritages seem to develop institutions which one way or another strive to guarantee fidelity to the original religious heritage.*

Most such institutions, whether they be a board of rabbis or the Sacred Congregation for the Protection of the Faith (as The Holy Office is now officially called) are concerned primarily with doctrinal propositions. Since doctrinal propositions are likely to change in response to major shifts in the creative imaginations of large numbers of the faithful, the institutions of review (to give them the most charitable possible name) are responding to changes brought about both by shifting philosophical and intellectual currents and by shifting currents in imagination. Such institutions seem necessary if only to declare when a story arrangement (symbol system) has gone beyond the paradigm of the privileged story, or when doctrinal assertions have gone utterly beyond the propositional limits of a heritage (for propositions have their historical development just as do images). But no institutional review, however effective, can contain the playful, manic, excited, creative dynamisms of the poetic imagination. Religious institutions might be better advised to monitor the activities of the creative imagination of their membership so as to understand what is the religious and human situation in which their people live (this process would once have been called "the discernment of spirits").

5.8 *Religious institutions suffer the same difficulties as do other institutions of transmitting instructions from the top which will be effectively carried out at the bottom.*

It is well known from organizational sociology that at each transmission point in a bureaucratic structure instructions may be subverted either deliberately because of disagreement, or inadvertently because of misunderstanding, selective perception, or fear of the implications of the instructions on one's own position. An order, for example, from the Pope may be almost unrecognizable by the time it reaches the parish priest or the congregation. Each transmission is a potential subversion mechanism in which deliberately or inadvertently an order may be disrupted or subverted. The top layer of leadership in religious organizations may be less aware than other organizational leadership of how difficult it is to effectively rule, especially in the absence of consent. President Kennedy was astonished during the Cuban missile crisis to discover that missiles he had ordered out of Turkey were still there. Perhaps the classic example of organizational subversion in recent religious history is the undermining of the decision of the encyclical, *Humanae vitae*. The Pope made a decision. The bishops accepted it, but did not attempt to impose it on parish priests, and parish priests in their turn either rejected the decision out of hand, or passed on the responsibility for the decision making to the married couples themselves.

The religious institution which exists to impose fidelity is often hard put to do so unless it has obtained consent from the membership.

Chapter Six
Belief Systems

Thus far I have discussed religion as the activity of the preconscious, prerational, or creative imagination or as poetic dynamisms of the personality. Experiences of grace renew our hopefulness. Residual images of those experiences persist in our imagination and influence our religious devotion, our religious attitudes, our religious behavior, social and political commitments, and our relationship with our spouses. However, in addition to being imagining creatures we are thinking creatures, and therefore we reflect on our religious images, unpack them, analyze them, criticize them, evaluate them, explain them, systematize them, and sort them out. Sometimes this exercise of the rational dimension of our personality is quick and intuitive. At other times it is far more elaborate and systematic. In our complex, modern world the tendency toward detailed and critical "unpacking" of the images is strong. However, even in more ancient times, formal religious reflection came very soon after the initial religious experience. The process of formally reflecting on experience is true both of the individual biographical experience and the historical experience of tradition.

6.1 *In reflecting on his religious imageries, the individual develops a "world view," a response to the critical problems of human suffering and death.*

The image is of Heaven as a paradise of pleasure and delight; the world view is the reaction of the total person, intellect included, through, let us say, news that a parent is going to die of a long and lingering illness. A warm "story of God" will more likely produce a more hopeful world view than the opposite. Thus, the warm religious imagery scale that we developed in our research on the young Catholic adults correlates above .3 with McCready's hopeful world view scale, and, when both partners of a marriage have warm religious images, correlation with them both having hopeful response to tragedy and death is in excess of .4.

6.2 *The world view is something more elaborate than a religious story. But it is also less elaborate than a doctrinal proposition. Doctrinal propositions and world views need not correlate.*

Thus, one might commit oneself intellectually to the proposition that the Scriptures are the word of God and not respond hopefully in the face of tragedy. A world view is a practical orientation of the rational dimensions of the personality. It gives a person a pattern of meaning with which to respond to life's most serious problems. A doctrinal proposition is a theoretical truth which in itself does not necessarily provide such a response.

6.3 *Religious images are a much stronger predictor of world view than is doctrinal orthodoxy.*

Propositions which exist independently of any grounding in the creative imagination are likely to have little impact on practical responses to suffering and tragedy. On the other hand, if doctrinal propositions are solidly linked to the religious imagination, they will have a considerable impact on world view. Thus, a Catholic doctrinal orthodoxy scale dealing with Papal primacy, Papal infallibility, and the sinfulness of missing a mass on Sunday related to a hopeful world view .10 level, while warm religious images related to a hopeful world view at a .40 level. There was only a small relationship between orthodoxy and imagery (.1). On the other hand, belief in life after death, which was linked to warm imagery by a .2 correlation, had an impact on hopefulness almost as strong as did the warm images (.27 versus .32). Some doctrinal propositions, however important they may be for the intellectual structure of faith, are unrelated either to religious images or to a response to tragedy, but others are powerfully related to both.

One hardly need say that from a point of view of social science research it is important to discover which doctrinal propositions seem to be related to both images and behavior, and which are unrelated.

6.4 *Religious images also tend to correlate more powerfully with social behavior and attitude than do doctrinal propositions.*

Some doctrinal propositions may have a direct influence on religious behavior. But if doctrinal propositions are not rooted in the creative imagination, they are not likely to have much effect on social commitment. The Catholic orthodoxy scales mentioned in the previous proposition did not relate significantly to a social commitment scale made up of feelings of aiding the poor, or working for racial justice, and for being concerned about community problems. But the warm religious imagery scale did relate significantly to the social commitment measure. Whether you believe in infallibility of the

Pope or the primacy of the Pope or the sinfulness of missing Sunday mass does not have any effect on your social involvement, but if you picture God as a lover and Heaven as a paradise of pleasures and delights, then you are likely to be more socially committed. Religious images have more impact on social attitudes and behaviors than do doctrinal propositions—according to our theory because they are anterior to the propositions and more powerful than the propositions.

6.5 *Those who first experience "founding events" normally articulate the experience initially in terms of a "symbol arrangement" which is readily available.*

I now turn from assertions about the relationship between image and belief systems for individuals to a consideration of how the religious experience which begins a heritage or a tradition is converted into a belief system. I will use the illustration of the development of early Christianity because it happens to be a process with which I am familiar. Data to support the description of the development of Christian belief systems from the primary "founding experience" to philosophical and theological elaboration can be found in the literature of early Christian history. Social scientists studying religious sects and cults could, I suspect, easily apply the same paradigm to the development of such groups.

The followers of Jesus experienced in the "Easter event" a shattering conviction that the Jesus who died still lived. To articulate this enormous event to themselves and to those to whom they wished to announce it, they turned to a "story arrangement" available in the Jewish tradition. Jesus was described as a "Messiah," a "prophet," a "suffering servant," a "son of man," a "Moses," a "David," an "Abraham" and an "Adam."

6.6 *However, rearrangements take place in this available system precisely because it is necessary to distinguish what is special and unique about "founding events."*

Jesus was a special kind of Messiah, not a political one, a special kind of Adam, a progenitor not of the old humanity, but a new humanity, a special kind of Moses leading the people out of spiritual rather than material slavery. The cues and the linkages among the symbols are already undergoing change. There is continuity between the founding event and previous religious experience, tradition and images. There also is a new rearrangement of stories, a new linkage of symbols.

6.7 *Very early, it becomes necessary to "explain" or "interpret" the symbolization. At this point, there is a change from poetry to prose, and reflective propositions.*

In the early chapters of the Acts of the Apostles one can see Peter and his colleagues already explaining, interpreting, arguing, answering. Not only is Jesus the risen one, the Messiah, the new Adam, the new Moses, the fulfiller of the Messianic prophecies, he is also the one who has been put to death by an horrendous mistake. The nature of and the reasons for this mistake—hardly anticipated by the Messianic prophecies—must be explained. Even if, as now seems generally to be agreed, the early chapters of Acts are substantially more theological than they are historical, it still seems likely that they represent a process that began very early.

It must be emphasized that there is no necessary infidelity to the original spirit in subsequent development. A trajectory is launched at the beginning of the experience which, given historical and cultural fact, leads if not with implacable logic, then with understandable evolution to subsequent development (such as the Councils of Chalcedon or Ephesus).

6.8 *At first many different interpretative systems emerge. They tend to converge in an integrated system.*

By the time one gets to the composition of the Christian Gospels one is already well into the process of informal philosophical and theological reflection. The Christology of the synoptic Gospels tends to be "quasi-adoptionist." Jesus was the man God assumed unto himself for his own purposes, whereas the Gospel of St. John has a much more "logos" Christology—Jesus is a preexisting deity linked with human nature. While they overlap somewhat, these two positions are distinct from one another, especially since Luke and Mark were rigorously resisting in their Gospels a notion current at the time of writing that Jesus was a kind of "God-man" of the sort encountered in Greek mythology. By the middle of the second century, the Johanine tradition emerged dominant, subsuming more or less within itself some of the elements of the synoptic tradition, but not without tension and conflicts.

6.9 *Then philosophical perspectives are adopted for explaining to disciplined reason the meaning contained in the prose text recounting the experience of the founding event.*

Toward the end of the second century, formal Greek philosophical models were applied to the Johanine Christology. Abstract concepts of "substance" and "nature" and "person" were introduced into the argument and imposed on the scriptural text and the antecedent experience. Just as poetry had become prose, so prose had become theology.

6.10 *Eventually a number of prose statements (or creeds) are developed to articulate clearly and precisely the meaning of the experience and the essentials for faith in that experience.*

The first four ecumenical councils of the Church—Nicea, Constantinople, Ephesus, and Chalcedon—were concerned with articulating in precise, Greek philosophical terminology the relationships between substance, person, and nature that a Christian must accept as the orthodox articulation of the meaning of the prose text of the Scriptures, which texts in return reflected the early symbolization of the primary experience and events. The route from Easter and "new Moses" to "homoousiss" and "homoiousious" is a long and intricate one. I do not intend to suggest that the path is invalid. Indeed, many scholars have shown how trajectories begun in very early times point accurately—given the philosophical environment of the era—to the creedal conclusions four centuries later. Nonetheless, a study of these first four centuries reveals some of the risks involved in detaching philosophical speculation from the primary religious experiences on which the speculation purports to be based.

There is a tension between creed and story. The former is too precise for the latter. The latter is variegated and too rich for the former. Both are inevitable in a religious heritage, though their different perspectives lead to the possibility of conflict—not merely conflict between different creeds based on different interpretations of the primary story, but also conflicts between creed believers and story believers. A belief system without creed may be too amorphous to survive in a propositional culture like our own. But a belief system without story may lack human vitality. Both story and creed are simple. The former is a direct result of the experience. Story is nothing more than an attempt to resonate and represent that experience, while creed, far removed from experience, is a result of philosophical refinement and purification and distillation of the experience.

6.11 *Reforms within religious heritages normally appeal either to early creedal statements or to the original symbolizations against more elaborate and/or rigidified doctrinal structures which are perceived as intervening between the purity of the past and the present condition.*

Almost always the reformer appeals either to the simple creed (which as we have seen evolved out of a not so simple process) or the simple truth of the Gospel (which is already a reflection on the original story and the basic experience). In the terms of the theoretical perspective I present in this book, the slogan "ecclesia semper reformanda" makes an extraordinary amount of sociological sense. One must return to the stories and to the original experience if one is to get to the raw, primal strength of a religious heritage. But one also needs reflection, even abstract speculation, if one is to humanly and reasonably live the implications of the story; a belief system must be articulated and then justified in the face of philosophical assaults.

However, it would appear that most reforms are not carried out, at least not directly, by new ideas or by new institutional reforms, but by modifications of human relationships. The Vatican Council, it would appear, has had its impact on Catholics through sympathetic parish priests, devout mothers, and skillfully passionate husbands.

In this chapter I have considered two different kinds of parallel developmental processes, both dealing with the creation of belief systems. In the individual person the religious experiences of his life (experiences which, of course, are shaped by the creedal and symbolic repertory he brings to the experience) become belief systems and personal creeds—which may or may not be intimately connected. For the historical heritage, experience becomes reflection, speculation, elaboration, systematicization, and finally distillation in the creeds and catechetic proposition. Both processes are religious and are an inevitable outcome of the endless dialogue between prerational and the rational that goes on in the human personality. The battle cry of reformers demanding "endless reformation" represents sociological wisdom both for the individual and for the tradition. While one may need the creeds, the catechisms, the philosophical elaborations, and the systematizations, all the vitality of personal religion and religious heritage depends ultimately on the raw, elementary, primal strength of experience and the story which articulates it.

Chapter Seven
Communion

There are three kinds of "communion" relationships in religion. One we have called vertical community—the believer's unity with the past through religious tradition, a tradition which is a belief system, a creed, and more basically, fundamentally and primordially, an arrangement of symbols, an interrelated network of stories. A second communion is unity between the believer and his contemporaries, a unity which is broader than the organizational structure that sustains it and which might be called a denomination or a church—or at the grass roots a parish or a congregation. In this sense the religious community is that group of persons who share the symbol arrangement, the belief system, the creedal propositions at a given time. I am postponing the consideration of this community as long as possible in this analysis in order to emphasize the "secularity" of religion; basic religious experiences, encounters with grace, and the symbols which resonate and represent these encounters are likely to occur outside the ecclesiastical situation and are logically and in some senses chronologically anterior to it. In the next chapter I will turn to a consideration of horizontal community—churches. I take it that this procedure is justified by the fact that religion existed a long time before there were churches, and that two of the three principal denominational aggregations in the United States, Catholicism and Judaism, came into existence as part of a religious heritage and in a religious cultural milieu in which the institutional structures were minimal in comparison with what they are today.

In this chapter I will deal with the third type of communion—unity with the otherness which was encountered in the experience of grace.

7.1 *Often the experience of goodness involves a feeling that one has been the object of communication. Often, also, it is felt that it is possible to communicate back to the other.*

Many experiences of otherness hint that the other will receive responses, indeed, may even be awaiting and demanding responses. No information exists to indicate what proportion of experiences of grace do hint at the possibility or even the necessity of response, though there is a correlation between ecstatic experience and prayer.

7.2 *Such communication may be called prayer, a common phenomenon in the human condition.*

In the United States prayer is almost universal, more than 90 percent of the population prays at least some of the time, 80 percent prays every week, 50 percent prays every day. More people pray weekly than are certain of the existence of God or are certain of life after death. Young men and young women pray at about the same rates, somewhat lower rates than older men and women. As the age increases, both men and women pray more, with the increase in women's prayer being sharper than the increase in men's prayer, apparently because the socio-emotional role of women makes them the "praying specialists" in the family. With the passage of time, too, there are more people to be prayed for, children and then grandchildren. Prayer correlates strongly with psychological well-being and also correlates (in two different and unrelated studies) with willingness to cooperate with survey interviewers (for further details on this subject, see the forthcoming work by Philip Morgan and Andrew Greeley, "Structures of Prayer")."

7.3 *The more powerful and vivid the story appears in the religious imagination, the stronger the propensity to prayer.*

Doctrinal or ethical orthodoxies are ineffectual predictors of prayerfulness. So are levels of religious education. The religious joyfulness of one's family of origin, however, does predict that one will pray frequently when one is an adult. An especially powerful relationship exists between the NORC warm image scale and frequency of prayer. There is, furthermore, a structural correlation between husband's prayer and wife's prayer (and vice-versa), and this relationship increases with time. Prayer, in other words, seems to be like religious imagery in that it is affected not by propositional education or by propositional orthodoxy, but by experiences, especially family experiences and religious and family experiences as these are mediated by warm religious images.

7.4 *When prayer becomes external and formal it may be called ritual.*

This proposition is definitional. "Private" prayer and public prayer are both attempts at responding to the otherness that has been experienced. Some solitary prayer may be sufficiently formal and externalized to be called ritual, and doubtless, ritual situations can enhance and reinforce private devotional orientation. It is not necessary in this presentation to determine whether ritual or private prayer comes first. In more primitive societies it may be that public, communal prayer is anterior to private prayer, and, indeed, there may be in such societies no private prayer. In a complex industrial society, particularly in the West where individualism is strongly emphasized, private devotion may be anterior to public devotion.

Prayer is probably the most understudied frequent human activity. Americans pray more often than they have sex, and prayer seems to correlate at much higher levels with psychological well-being than does sex. An enormous literature exists reporting on research on the sex life of Americans. No attention at all has been paid to their prayer life.

There is also a positive correlation between frequency of prayer and sexual fulfillment in marriage.

7.5 *Prayer and ritual are often designed not merely to respond to communication but to produce communion, that is, an experience of unity with the previously perceived goodness.*

There are two testable assertions in the above proposition. The first is that prayer sometimes is designed to produce communion—that is, to replicate the experience of hopefulness. One deliberately goes into a prayer situation seeking to establish a linkage with the otherness that was encountered in the grace experience. The second assertion is that, in fact, prayer and/or ritual do, indeed, sometimes replicate more or less strongly the original experience of grace.

The first subproposition is definitional. While many private prayers, it seems safe to assume, are not explicitly intended to reproduce an experience of grace, many formal religious rituals with their strong emphasis on the basic symbols of a religious heritage seem explicitly and deliberately designed to reproduce at least a hint of prior experience. Fire and water, for example, in the Roman Catholic Easter ritual and the lighting of the Easter candle in a darkened church are clearly meant to recall past experiences in the life of the congregants as well as the founding experience of the religious heritage.

The second subproposition requires empirical investigation. There is no reason to doubt that occasionally experiences of hope are replicated in prayer situations, particularly in the ecstasy caused by public ritual (It is in the "effervescence" of public ritual that Emile Durkheim locates the origins of religion. I would agree that in moments of joyousness during public ritual there is an encounter of grace and an experience of hopefulness and an awareness of otherness. I would not, however, accept Durkheim's implication that this collective effervescence is the only experience of grace in the human condition. I would concede, however, that it is or can be a spectacular experience of grace.). We know from biography that extraordinary things happen even in the modern world to individuals caught up in the drama of public ritual—the conversion of the poet and diplomat Paul Claudel at the first vespers of Christmas in Notre Dame de Paris, for example. We also know from NORC research that moments of prayer are one of the common times when ecstatic or religious experiences do occur. In any systematic and serious study of prayer we would want to know under what circumstances private and public do, indeed, lead to a replication of experiences of grace, or minimally strengthening and validating of the hopefulness encountered in such experiences. Under what conditions, in other words, does prayer seem to renew hope? One must speculate that it does so a fair amount of the time. Otherwise people would not pray so much.

7.6 *Prayer and ritual involve the poetic dimension of the personality precisely because they are designed to reproduce an earlier experience which impacted on the poetic capacity (creative imagination, preconscious).*

There is virtually nothing in the research literature that enables us to confirm the expectation that prayer is imaginative activity, since we know almost nothing about how people pray. NORC data enables us to make the following observations: Two-thirds of our sample (Catholics under thirty) pray with their own words, 26 percent offer prayers of petition, a third pray often to specific persons, a fifth often use formal prayers, a little more than half offer prayers of gratitude, only 7 percent use the Bible for reflection, two-fifths pray for meaning in life, 5 percent use music as a prayer aid, 7 percent pray often on their knees, and about half pray informally.

Historians of religion and anthropologists have analyzed the role of public ritual in the life of primitive and archaic peoples. Mircea Eliade contends that religious ritual links the great paradigmatic events by which the Gods imposed order on chaos *in illo tempore*. The ritual is a reenactment of the paradigmatic battle between the forces of order and chaos. It links that battle with the daily struggle in the lives of the people contending against chaos as they plow their fields, protect their crops, and ward off attacks from the outside on their village or camp.

The camp, particularly the center of the camp, which was taken to be a link between earth and Heaven, represents order. The dangerous world beyond the camp or the village is chaos. The ritual festival links the people to the paradigmatic events, motivates them to continue the effect of such events by sharing in them by extending the boundaries of order against chaos. Oftentimes, it also provides instructions on how the work is to be done—giving precise orders, for example, concerning the sowing of seeds.

Fertility rituals link the divine fertility with the fertility of the fields. Oftentimes men and women would sleep together in the newly planted fields to insure that the fertility of the gods would be linked with the fertility of their crops (a practice which in some European countries seems to have continued—for one reason or another!—even to the twentieth century).

Eliade's interpretation is not necessary for the theory expounded in this volume. However, it does illustrate how anthropology and the history of religions confirm the imaginative dimension of ritual. Conceptual and propositional religion seems to have barely existed in many times and places. The Christian religious heritage passes itself on for the first millennium and a half with a minimal of formal propositional religious education through stories, pictures, music, stained-glass windows, and religious festivals, all aimed at the imaginative dimension of the human personality, and sustained by a symbolic arrangement with only a minimal oversight from creedal propositions.

7.7 *Therefore, ritual not only disposes toward communion, but is also a powerful institution of religious socialization.*

Ritual does not teach religious truths; it passes on religious symbols and stories and the experiences of hopefulness contained in these stories (as well as symbol systems or arrangements). This transmission does not necessarily involve the logic of a discursive intellect, but follows the logic of the preconceptual imagination.

7.8 *Ritual is also a form of play and, hence, reflects the "hilarity" of otherness.*

The scholars who have studied play define it as an activity that occurs in a social and personal environment which has been established distinct from the environment of everyday life, and regulated by rules and assumptions which are peculiar to it and distinctive from the rules and assumptions of everyday life. The elaborate regulations and behavior patterns, say, of a professional football game or of a renaissance court are manifestations of play, of a world of "make believe." Religious ritual also creates its own world in which the creative imagination is freed from the obligations of everyday routine to create a "make believe" environment in which one may encounter otherness (make believe, of course, does not here mean fictional or false). The incongruity of grown men and women bowing and scraping in the court of Versailles or at an old Catholic solemn high mass, or for that matter, in an athletic game puts the activity on the borderline of the humorous, if not to all the participants and observers, at least to some of them. Hilarity and dead seriousness are not necessarily opposed to one another. Think, for example, of the wide receiver during his celebratory dance in the end zone before he "spikes" the football. Precisely because it is playful in the sense of being a free creation in the world of make believe ritual, it inevitably skirts the hilarious and on occasion slips over into the burlesque. However, since otherness is on occasion experienced as hilarious, the hilarity of each ritual is not totally unacceptable to the ritualists.

While there are historical and anthropological analyses of the play and hilarity aspects of religious behavior, there has been no research on the role of play in contemporary American religious activity. The theoretical positions taken in this book would predict that since the creative imagination, uncontrolled or at least not completely inhibited by the discursive intellect, endlessly plays with the mass of images at its disposal, there will be substantial play aspects in any religious activity.

To state the same expectation another way, the preconceptual personality operates in an environment of "make believe" in which images can be juxtaposed and rearranged the way they are, for example, in dreams or in poetry. Religious sensibility is not the same as either dream or poetry (in the strict sense of the word). Yet, it is a similar sensibility, and, hence, can be expected to be playful. Given the fact that in playing there are often incongruous juxtapositions, hilarity also seems inevitable in religion.

7.9 *When rituals become ritualized they have less effectiveness both at renewing experiences of grace and passing on symbol systems.*

While the ritual may originally be created as an act of spontaneous play, it very easily and, perhaps inevitably, becomes ritualized, formal, routine, unchangeable, and rigidly constrained by regulation. It then has much less power to excite the imagination, to recall past experiences, to revitalize and renew hopefulness and to reinvest with religious energy the symbol objects it contains within its ceremonial. Such weakened ritual may not have lost all of its ability to renew experiences of hope and to transmit religious heritages, but its power has certainly diminished. Often it seems it can do nothing more than stir up a vague sense of the mysterious or at least of mystification, which may produce some sense of wonder in the participants. Religious reformers will frequently call for the renewal of ritual forms, risking criticisms from both conservatives and radicals that they are destroying the sense of the mysterious and the sacred in religious activity (thus, both anthropologist Lionel Tiger and dissident Catholic Archbishop Marcel LeFevbre are opposed to the liturgy in the vernacular languages, and on the same grounds the sense of mystery, they contend, is lost when the sacred is dealt with in the profane languages). Jewish reformers (with a small "r") who attempt to put the Sabaoth ritual into the vernacular languages encounter the same opposition.

The process of the routinization of the charismatic is well known in the social science literature. In this volume we need not pause to discuss the reasons why the means of ritual ceremony are converted into ends in themselves. Although from the point of view of the theory of religion proposed in this book, it must be said that mystery is not the same as obscurity, and that what may be mystifying and mysterious to some may also be deadly boring to others.

There are no data to indicate that ritualized ritual has less renewing or socializing impact than does somewhat freer and more spontaneous ritual. Surely, however, the spontaneous liturgies of the various charismatic movements and cults and sects studied by various contemporary sociologists of religion seem to produce more vigorous reaction in their congregants than do the stately formal liturgies of the older and established churches. Indirect evidence is available from the overwhelming support of the American Catholics—despite Professor Tiger—of the vernacular liturgy (almost nine-tenths support the change).

7.10 *Precisely because prayer is an action linking the story of one's own life to the overarching story, one can expect correlations between prayer and various measures of psychological well-being.*

In fact NORC research shows that frequent prayer correlates positively with psychological well-being, with sexual fulfillment in marriage, with general marital satisfaction, and even with willingness to cooperate with interviewers who are conducting survey interviews. However, this correlation seems to be specified by prayers of gratitude, for it exists only among those who say they offer prayers of gratitude "often." Thus, it would appear that when prayer relates the story of one's own life to the overarching story in a way that leaves one open to the grace contained in the overarching story does prayer contribute to personal happiness.

7.11 *The more benign and graceful the stories of God in a person's religious imagination, the more likely he/she is to pray frequently.*

As noted previously, doctrinal propositions do not lead to more frequent prayer. But images of God, particularly of

God as a mother and lover, correlate powerfully with frequent prayer.

If creedal propositions and doctrinal formulation and ecclesiastical structure must be in order to insure their dynamic vitality, then the dynamic vitality must be subject to the injunction "sempre formanda" so must liturgy. Rituals that lose touch with the raw and primal power of the preconceptual imagery which originally generated will have little capacity to renew and replicate those experiences. It does not follow that ritual need always be "low church" and that all masses need to be guitar masses. To put the matter at its most practical guitar masses can become routinized and ritualized even more quickly, one suspects, than solemn high liturgies. But, all liturgies must stir the imagination and renew, however moderately, experiences of hopefulness or the congregation will be tempted to fall asleep.

Chapter Eight
Horizontal Community

Churches or denominations are the institutional structures of religious communities. Religion cannot be reduced to the ecclesiastical or the denominational but is capable of permeating all aspects of human life. NORC research evidence shows that some intense religious experiences do, indeed, occur in the physical buildings that are worship centers for denominations, and some even during denominational services. However, experiences which renew hope occur more frequently in nondenominational settings. Grace can be encountered by those who have no denominational settings available. Religion may occur in church, in other words, but it need not do so.

Nevertheless, churches or denominations are a normal result of religious experiences in our contemporary, complex industrial society. Churches are brought into being by experiences of hope. Whatever other purpose they may serve, one of their purposes will always remain to facilitate renewals of hopefulness.

8.1 *There is a tendency to share an experience of goodness with others so that the experience can be articulated for oneself and validated by others.*

The personal interviews that William McCready has done with those who have had intense religious experiences demonstrate that not all such experiences are shared. Many individuals keep their dramatic encounters with grace completely secret, fearing ridicule or misunderstanding if they attempt to share their good news with others. Therefore, no claim can be made that all experiences of hopefulness are automatically shared with others. Patently, many of them are, whether they be the apostles' Easter experience of Jesus perceived by them as not dead, but alive, or the marriage encounter couples' enthusiastic proclamation of how much their week-end enrichment experience has meant for marital happiness.

8.2 *In some cases the support of others is perceived as essential for responding to the demands goodness makes.*

In such cases one shares the good news not merely for the joy of proclaiming it, but also for gaining the support of those to whom it is proclaimed. The good news of hopefulness in these conditions is perceived as demanding that one make converts—"even unto the ends of the earth." The grace which is encountered is imagined as requiring, or requesting, or at least wanting not merely the response of the individual who has experienced grace, but the response of others and, indeed, the response of everyone. Otherness is pictured as comprehensive in its demands. The techniques of persuading others to join in one's response may run from gentle proclamation to moral force to the sword.

Not all experiences of grace require that one make converts, either to please the Wonderful or to validate the experience of wonder. All that is asserted in the present proposition is that some hope-renewing experience will lead to the formation and the development of religious community. The proposition is, indeed, an empirical one, but there is so much evidence of its validity that it seems reasonable to assume that no further research documentation is required.

8.3 *A principal function of the religious community is to provide an interpretation for individual and, perhaps, collective
hope-renewing experiences.*

Communities can emerge in one of two ways. A number
of individuals may share a common experience or one person
may so effectively proclaim his own experience that others
join him, either seeking the same experience or perceiving
that they have already encountered a similar renewal of hope
themselves. In both cases there is a powerful propensity to
find an interpretation of the experience which will link the
members of the group together. "Your experience" and "my
experience" then can truly be "our experience." The interpretation will in all likelihood initially be quite simple, little
more than retelling of the story with the most simple of propositional meanings (belief systems) imposed on it, so that
the link between it and the overarching explanation of the
purpose of the cosmos and of human life may be clear. Your
"story" and my "story" merged into "our story" are briefly
and simply linked to the "Big Story."

When the stage of seeking an interpretation for shared experiences is reached, then a religious community begins to
take shape and form. It is the turning point when a relatively
amorphous collection of enthusiasms cross the boundary
line, and an unstructured collectivity begins to become a
structured community. The road from Jerusalem to the
Roman Curia begins to be traveled.

I take it that there is sufficiently adequate data both in the
history of religion and the studies of the development of the
Christian Church and in the sociological research currently
on sects and cults to confirm the validity of this proposition,
at least as the process of community formation is concerned.
My contention that the primary step is the articulation of a
common interpretation is submitted as an hypothesis
especially for the study of cults and sects.

8.4 *Communities of interpretation grow and develop according to the dynamic which affects the growth and development of any human group from the simple collectivity to a complex organization.*

The literature in sociology of religion is filled with studies of the "routinization of the charisma" as the groups move from cult to sect to established sect to denomination and, perhaps, to a church, with a wide variety of variations, transitions, sidepaths, and tangents in the process. Indeed, it would not be altogether wrong to say the whole sub-field of organizational studies began at the turn of the century with the ideal type comparison between sect and church. There is no point in this book in repeating or even summarizing the voluminous literature, save to note as I have done previously in *The Denominational Society* that the distinction between sect and church as a research tool ought not to be considered a description of most American religious groupings. Even the most elaborate of high church denominations have many sect-and cult-like groups within them, as for example, charismatic movements in Roman Catholicism and Episcopalianism. In a society like ours even the most enthusiastic small religious group quickly develops patterns of institutionalization. In *The Denominational Society* I said that institutionalization begins when the first mimeograph machine is purchased. I would now have to say when the first Xerox copier is purchased.

As the interpretative group grows and as routine behavior patterns are established, the organized collectivity, once a means to the end of renewing and reinforcing experiences of hope, may become an end in itself. Institutional problems take on an importance which may at times minimize or even exclude the primary goal of sustaining the memory and reenacting and reproducing the first graced experience. Yet, even in the most rigid and most institutionalized church, it is rare for the primary goal to disappear completely; and the interpretation of shared or common experiences of grace continues to occur. An important research issue and one to which little attention has been paid is the capacity of the primary religious goal to survive "routinization" and intermittently to reassert itself through reform movements. I have argued in *The Denominational Society* that in the United States religious denominations, when they establish their own colleges and seminaries and their own publications, they in effect produce a critical and intellectual class which is a countervailing power within the institution against institutionalization—even though their existence is in itself a result of institutionalization.

8.5 *Religious communities exist, therefore, to replicate, enhance, validate, interpret and reaffirm past experiences of goodness and presuppose for future experiences.*

This proposition is definitional, a summary of the previous propositions in this chapter and a location of the religious community (or "Church") in the theory of religion being presented in this book. The research challenge indicated by this proposition is to determine under what circumstances a religious community does fulfill the primary purpose that the proposition asserts it has. It would also be interesting to learn what proportions of time and resource in a denomination are devoted to this goal.

8.6 *The religious community itself can both trigger hope-renewing experiences and act as a symbol of such an experience.*

Though "church" is not a primal symbol like water or fire or oil or food or sex, it can assume enormous importance in the life of a person, especially when it is merely a religious dimension of a broader community structure. The church as communion of all the faithful becomes an image in the preconscious and a "story of grace" to articulate experiences and to link "my" story with the Big Story. Unfortunately, and perhaps unconscionably, in our research on religious symbols we did not think to discover what images of church the respondent stored in his preconscious. It does not seem unreasonable to assume, however, that a "warm" image of church (church as a "lover" or as a "mother") would be an important picture in the religious imagination.

8.7 *In some societies, especially simple ones, the religious community is not distinct from the basic social realities of family and tribe.*

We can leave it to the anthropologists and the archeologists to describe the level of social complexity necessary to produce a distinctive religious organization within a society, and also the extent to which even in simple societies relationships and behavior patterns are experienced as distinctively religious. it is sufficient to assert here that a distinctive and specifically religious subculture does not seem to be an absolute social necessity. Religion does not necessarily produce churches.

8.8 *In other and more complex societies the community of interpretation may take on institutional existence separate from the tribe and the family. Nevertheless, tribe and, particularly, family continue to play an important role in both horizontal religious community and as a link in vertical community.*

The second part of this proposition is decisive. It is a mistake to assume—as some students of religion apparently assume—that once the church comes into existence the family and the tribe relinquish their religious function. On the contrary, tribe and family are often intermediaries between an individual and other individuals in the presently existing community of interpretation, and, also, mediating links between the individual and the religious heritage which has been handed down from the past. Quite simply, the individual learns within the family both what he is religiously (Protestant, Catholic, Jew, etc.) and what the religious identification means. Family, as we shall see in a subsequent chapter, is the religious socializer *par excellence*. But the family passes on a religious tradition which has been shaped and formed by the tribal experience (ethnic background) of which a given family is a part. The Catholicism passed on by an Irish Catholic family is not the same as the Catholicism passed on by an Italian Catholic family.

8.9 *The family is normally more important than the church, both as a community of religious heritage and a community of current religious interpretation.*

This proposition is true both with regard to the transmission of religious doctrine and religious devotions and with regard to the transmission of belief systems and religious stories or images. Though formal religious education may make an impact on the religious socialization process, the family religious environment seems to be more important, particularly in the transmission of religious images. It is precisely those who come from "warm" families who are most likely to have the warmest religious images. Those who come from hopeful families are more likely to have the most hopeful belief systems. But, the family's hopefulness and religious imagery, in turn, are affected to some extent by the ethnic subtradition of which the family is a part.

The data to support these assertions in various NORC research enterprises are overwhelming. As we shall see in the subsequent chapters, McCready is able to explain more than half of the variation in religious behavior of adolescents without having recourse to any items on the adolescent questionnaire, relying purely on information about the religious behavior of the adolescents' parents and, particularly, the religious behavior of the father.

It is more useful to conceptualize the family as being a part of the church, or even as agent for the church in religious socialization. The church passes on an interpretation of the common religious symbols mostly through its families, though the families may make additions and subtractions and special interpretations of their own about which the church would be less than enthusiastic.

8.10 *When church, tribe, and family fail to act as communities of religious transmission and interpretation, other collectivities will tend to fill the vacuum.*

This assertion is intended to summarize the evidence available in the current literature on religious sects and cults. The membership in these groups is disproportionally recruited from families where there is either no religious affiliation, or a technical and formal religious affiliation devoid of religious conviction. I would suggest to those engaged in such research that the most likely recruits for such movements are those whose inherited religious affiliation (or inherited agnosticism) provide no powerful religious story, no opportunity to experience renewal of hopefulness, and no image to articulate and represent such experiences when they occur.

8.11 *In a highly differentiated society there is a strong tendency for religious congruence in primary group relationships.*

I am assuming in this proposition that persons are more at ease with those who share the same religious stories and basic beliefs, and, hence, they selectively recruit for their primary groups those who share such stories. I further assume that, once an intimate relationship has been established, the intimacy of the relationship itself draws those who are in it toward common religious symbols and interpretation. I submit that not only do primary groups reinforce and validate religious orientations and beliefs, they also depend on shared beliefs to maintain their unity and to deal with their problems, and there is, therefore, enormous pressure within a primary group for religious conformity, that is to say, for shared experience, shared symbols, shared ritual, shared stories, and shared belief systems.

There are three bits of empirical evidence available to us that support this proposition:

A. Though many things changed between 1963 and 1974, in NORC studies of American Catholics at both times, three-quarters of American Catholics reported that their three closest friends were Catholics. The tendency, in other words, to choose close friends from within one's own religious denomination survives despite enormous declines in devotional practice and sexual and doctrinal orthodoxy.

B. While marriage across denominational lines is a frequent phenomenon, (the evidence is presently inconclusive as to whether the phenomenon is increasing)* there is a tendency for religious change, or conversion, or "musical chairs" to take place in association with marriage, so that at least denominational homogeneity is guaranteed to the family. Normally the change is in the direction of the denomination of the more devout partner.

---

*The young Catholics in the 1979 NORC study were more likely to engage in religiously mixed marriages than their parents, though it appeared this was in substantial part the result of a decline in pressure for the non-Catholic partner to convert. Interestingly enough, the religious

C. Religious mixed marriages do not seem to have a harmful effect on the religious practice of Catholics (at any rate), only if the Catholic comes from a devout family and marries a devout spouse. Similarly, the rebound in a marriage toward the end of the first decade of married life occurs in a religiously mixed marriage only if husband and wife share the same intense religious imagery.

D. In the NORC study, *The Young Catholic Family*, we established that religious imagery converges as the marriage develops, especially if the marital relationship is a satisfactory one. We are in no position to say whether converging of religious imagery is a cause or an effect of marital satisfaction (and presumably causality flows in both directions), but for our purposes here it is enough to point out that in the primary group the pressure for religious homogeneity affects not only denominational affiliation, but even basic religious imagery.

E. During the course of a marriage the religious images of husband and wife tend to affect one another; the correlations between husband's score and wife's score on the scales measuring the various religious stories increase with the duration of the marriage.

8.12 In the modern world, churches are voluntary organizations, which means that leadership's power is based largely on its ability to obtain consent.

8.13 Hence, it is very easy for members to adhere to a tradition, a heritage, a community, and even an organization and still re-

---

mixed marriages conducted by Catholics occurred among those who married before they were twenty-five. There were rather few mixed marriages among those Catholics who were married after twenty-five.

ject either an important doctrinal or difficult ethical proposition.

Especially since the birth-control encyclical, the behavior of American Catholics sustains these two propositions. Over nine-tenths of the Catholic population reject the birth-control teaching, and three-quarters are not certain about Papal infallibility. Yet, despite a sharp decline in church attendance in the late 1960s and early 1970s, there has been little formal breaking away from Catholicism and, indeed, in the late 1970s there was a substantial upturn in church attendance. The crisis precipitated by the Vatican Council and by the birth-control encyclical apparently persuaded American Catholics that they were indeed members in a voluntary organization, and that no one could force them to participate in the organization in ways that they did not deem appropriate.

8.14 *The closer a religious influence is to where a person lives (and, indeed, to where he sleeps) the more impact it will have on his religious life.*

Parent and spouse are the most important religious influences, as we will note subsequently, and after them the parish clergy. Indeed, for Catholic young adults twice as much variance in religious identification could be explained by the quality of Sunday sermons than could be accounted for by all the "mass media" and "issues" combined—birth control, divorce, abortion, ordination of women, and Papal leadership.

To single out the two most important theoretical themes in this chapter: religious communities emerge as collectivities seeking to provide a common interpretation for shared experiences of grace. Even when they become highly institutionalized and rigidly structured there is still a tendency for some of this interpretative function to continue. Secondly, while the church does socialize directly through its formal teachings in school catechisms, sermons, and other such methods, its principal agent of religious socialization is the family; all the other techniques and methods of passing on the heritage and providing a common interpretation must be deemed as little more than auxiliary to what happens in the family environment.

Chapter Nine
Society

The relationship between religion and society has been hotly debated in the literature of the sociology of religion. Much of the heat has not generated light mostly because the combatants persisted in searching for a single model that would explain the relationships between religion and society at all times and all places. Thus, it would seem that much of the current discussion about America's "civil religion" (a discussion that is singularly uninhibited by the total absence of empirical data on the subject) would appear to be an attempt to apply to contemporary America—with very little attempt at nuance—Durkheim's theory of religion as the binding force of society. Robert K. Merton's sensible comment that sometimes religion is social adhesive and sometimes social solvent does not seem to have any impact on the civil religion discussion, not even to the extent of drawing to the attention of the participants that the American creed, based as it is in revolution, has always had socially disruptive potentialities.

The perspective taken in this book necessitates that I occupy a middle ground between those who see religion as a validator of established social order and those who see it as a threat to established orders (at least as a set of beliefs which *ought* to be a threat to the social order). I must emphasize mutuality and reciprocity of influence between religious stories and other social stories, and see that religious symbol systems both influence and are influenced by the other symbol systems which constitute a given culture. I must be wary, on the one hand, of those who see the religious stories as utterly subservient to the other stories, either in the most simple society or in the society with the most effectively established church. On the other hand, I also must be skeptical of the possibility of religious stories always standing in critique of the rest of society. The experience of grace is an unique experience *par excellence* and never can be subsumed completely within established cultural categories simply because that which is encountered is otherness. Religious encounters are by definition different. The stories about such encounters are necessarily distinctive stories. But the person who comes to the encounter has already been shaped not merely by the preexisting stories of his religious heritage, but by the overarching stories (or symbol systems) which underpin the social structure and the culture of his society. The American's encounter with grace, which renews his hopefulness and which seems to promise him "redemption," is bound to some extent to be influenced by the themes in our cultural tradition of political redemption and America as a nation with a redeeming mission. Furthermore, political and religious redemption can be so identified in the mind of Americans that the two become virtually the same. The public piety of the Carter years in the White House is rightwing evidence of this identification. The preenial support of the current fashion in social causes by liberal clergy provides evidence of the same phenomenon from the left.

9.1 *In simple, undifferentiated societies there is little distinction between religious stories and other social stories. Religion, nevertheless, is not completely identified with the social order. In more differentiated societies religious stories emerge as clearly distinctive religious symbols and social symbols interact with one another in mutually influencing directions. Finally, in complex and highly differentiated societies like our own, religious stories have only an indirect influence on social* *stories through their influence in shaping the perspectives and the world views of individuals and families.*

This proposition is intended to summarize the Parsons-Luckmann debate over the influence of religion. Both debators agreed on the tendency toward the differentiation of religion and the rest of the social order as society grows more complex. They differed on whether the indirect influence of religion on the rest of society through its world-view shaping role for individuals was major or minor. Both accepted, in other words, a "secularization" model of differentiation. But Luckmann thought that differentiation made religion unimportant, and Parsons felt that religion continued to be important, even if it exercises influence indirectly on large corporate structures.

Two comments on this debate seem appropriate. First of all, in less differentiated societies—both Parsons and Luckmann seem to have in mind societies where there were established churches or established religions—religion may have had less direct influence on life than either Parsons or Luckmann thought. The pieties, for example, of medieval and early modern monarchs never did seem to get in the way of their political plans. Nor did the religious commitment of businessmen interfere with their business activities. Secondly, the resurgence of militant and fundamentalist Islam, most notably in Iran, would suggest that the world has not evolved to a situation where it is totally impossible to have a theocracy.

Nonetheless, the Parsons-Luckmann differentiation model is useful and generally acceptable, so long as differentiation is not seen as a simple unidirectional, evolutionary dynamic. The appropriate stance for the social researcher is not to ask whether religion is less important in contemporary societies. The stories that articulate and represent the experiences of the renewal of hope are always important because they have an enormous impact on human behavior, an impact which is documentable and has, indeed, in some of our research at NORC been documented. The proper question, rather, is how in a given situation the mutuality of influence between religious stories and other social stories is working: How does religious imagery interact with other imagery? In a society like our own, where there is an enormous variety of religious and political symbols, the question becomes one of specifying for which kinds of people, which links exist between religious symbols and other social symbols: what kinds of stories of God tend to reinforce the social order, and what kind tend to lead, if not to disruption of the social order, at least to attempts to renew it. Such an analysis would be intricate and very expensive. This proposition begins with no *a priori* assumption about the direction of influence between religion and society.

9.2 *The flow of influence between religion and the rest of the society is reciprocal.*

9.3 *In some circumstances religious stories and religious groupings validate and confirm the dominant social perspective. In other circumstances religious stories and religious groupings are at odds with the dominant perspective, and they even explicitly attempt to destroy it.*

Religion influences the shape of the social structure through its impact on the individual's view of the purpose of his/her life and through the ethical imperatives (how important is industry and frugality, for example), which follow from the religious world view. This proposition is indebted to Max Weber, who ably refuted in his study of the Protestant ethic the Marxist notion that religion is simply a superstructure reflecting the values of the industrial structure of society. Weber did not deny the determining power of a society's economic organization, but he asserted that religion also had determining power. The question for research scholars, then, is to sort out the intricate relationships between religious stories and economic stories, and religious belief systems and economic belief systems, and religious institutions and economic institutions. The perspective taken in this book implies no *a priori* hypotheses about which way the influence flow will go in any specific situation. It does, however, imply that the researcher must look not merely at the influences of denominational affiliation, but also and especially at the influence of religious imagery on economic structure. The Irish and Italian and then Polish Catholics who migrated to the United States, for example, ought not, if one took the Protestant ethic theory literally, been particularly powerfully motivated for economic achievement. Despite their denominational affiliation, they have all passed the average American northern white Protestant in economic achievement. Nonetheless, there was, indeed, a religious effect in the achievement of the ethnic groups. The factor had little to do with denominational affiliation or propositional conviction and a lot to do with religious stories, particularly the linking of the faith story with the immigration story. The emphasis on educational and economic achievement in Catholic schools repeatedly demonstrated in NORC research is, I think, to be attributed precisely to the link in the imaginations of so many of us between faith and achievement in a combined story of "immigrant pilgrimage." The ethical imperatives of the story were clear: "prove that you can be a good American (which, of course, meant an economically successful American) and at the same time a good Catholic."

There is reason to expect considerable influence of religion on economic and social structures, precisely because religious stories seem almost inevitably to affect the other stories in a person's life, since the religious stories deal with life's ultimate goal and purpose. The Protestant ethic as Protestant may no longer exist. But one would suspect that religious stories do influence work ethics. NORC data established that religious stories have an effect on both social commitment and marital adjustment A religious researcher operating out of the perspective urged in this volume would be sensitive to the flow of influence from religion to other social institutions.

9.4 *Society influences religion especially because the institutions and relationships of society shape the "receiving apparatus" with which a person comes to his experience of otherness.*

The Other is more likely to be perceived in the western world as "personal" than he/she/it is in the East (though one must be careful of such a generalization for there are certain Hindu traditions in which the Other is imagined as a "Thou"). American racial, religious, and ethnic groups have different belief systems and different image patterns. Poles and Hispanics, for example, score somewhat higher than do other Catholic groups on the "warm" religious imagery scale, and the Irish score higher than other Catholics, the Swedes higher than other Protestants on measures of a hopeful world. Among Catholic groups the Irish also have the highest scores on a scale "passionate" and "story" of Mary the mother of Jesus, a score which can be explained by the greater propensity to the feminist's perspective among the Irish ethnic group. (The Irish also do well on measures of fatalism. In the Irish religious heritage fatalism and hope are not necessarily opposed.) Few sociologists would question the capacity of social structure to influence religious convictions and behaviors, though little careful attention has been paid to analyzing how these influences operate beyond simplistic assertions that the affluent are more likely to be religious because religion underpins the social order, or that the poor are more likely to be religious because religion is a way or coping with social deprivation. In fact, in American society there is relatively little correlation between religious behavior and social class. With the emergence of upper-middle-class charismatic movements there is also little relationship between social class and religious Enthusiasm. Most of the work of linking religious imagery with political, economic, and social imagery remains to be done.

There is some tentative explanation from apparent evidence that while there is little difference between Catholics and Protestants in their story of God, there is a slight propensity for Protestants to have a more stern and demanding story of Jesus than do Catholics.

9.5 *Society itself can be both an occasion of religious experience and a symbol for articulating experiences of grace.*

Such rituals as the coronation of a monarch, the inauguration of a President, the burial of a former President, national festivals such as the Fourth of July, Memorial Day, or the Bicentenial can for some people be an occasion for the renewal of hope. Commitment to the social and political story of a nation can serve as an articulation and a representation of an encounter with grace. The researchable question is how often such phenomena do, in fact, occur. In the extensive and often passionate debate about America's civil religion, no one has bothered to collect empirical data on the extent to which the political religion actually exists in the creative imagination of American citizens. All sides of the controversy seem to take for granted that such religio-politico imagery does, in fact, exist, and it does, in fact, affect the attitudes and behaviors in the political order of Americans. I have seen only one empirical attempt to evaluate this assumption (in an article sent to me for review which, despite my recommendation, was never published; hence, I cannot provide the name of the authors). It found no conformation at all for the civil religion thesis that the

American political system has become a quasi-religious object which is "worshipped" by many Americans.

Bellah's analysis of the religious images and pictures in presidential inaugural addresses and Lloyd Warner's earlier analysis of the religious imagery in American festivals such as Memorial Day and the Fourth of July are excellent sociological exercises. Unfortunately, no one has yet documented the strength of this imagery in the imagination of ordinary Americans or its impact on their attitudes and behaviors. I suspect that, save on special occasions, the civil religion is not nearly as important to most Americans as it is to those who debate about it.

Chapter Ten
Family

I will begin this chapter with four propositions which summarize assertions made previously and apply these assertions to the family.

10.1 *The family is the primary group "par excellence." All propositions made about primary group and religion in the previous section are "a fortiori" applicable to the family.*

10.2 *The family is the key community of religious transmission because the basic religious symbol arrangement in the preconscious seems to occur in the early childhood socialization process.*

10.3 *It is also often the family which transmits the preliminary interpretation of the symbols and the simple creedal formularies of religious heritage.*

10.4 *There is, however, no guarantee of harmony among symbol arrangement, creed and interpretation signals which a child receives.*

William McCready's research has solidly documented the validity of the "socialization" approach to religion. More than half of the variance in the religious behavior of adults can be explained by variables reflecting the religious behavior of their parents. The findings are replicated in the religious transmission from parents to teen-age children. McCready's research deals mostly with devotional measures and belief systems. However, my own investigation of religious symbols demonstrates that the religious joyousness of the family (more than mere religious devotion of the family) influences the religious imagery of the family member and through that image his world view, prayer, and social and political commitment. Social class and social deprivation theories have only trivial explanatory powers compared to the overwhelming power of the socialization model. Family experience does not, of course, completely determine religious behavior. A model which explains half of the variance is a very successful model in social research. Nonetheless, it leaves half of the variance unexplained and, hence, leaves room for many other influences to intervene in affecting the religious images, world views, beliefs, and devotional practice of adults. Nevertheless, McCready's work establishes beyond any doubt that a sociology of religion which ignores family influence is seriously deficient.

Inconsistency is possible between the imagery a child acquires and the creedal propositions that are transmitted to him. A child, for example, may be taught that there is no God. Still, he may approach adulthood with a repertory of warm symbols which represent experiences of renewed hopefulness for him and predispose him to other such symbols. On the other hand, a child may carry fundamentally negative and pessimistic stories in his preconscious and still articulate, if not a hopeful world view, at least doctrinally orthodox creedal or catechetical propositions which are at odds with his religious imagery. There is a strain toward consistency among imagery, world view, and doctrinal orthodoxy, but the strain is, by no means, irresistible. Further research will be required to sort out the intricate relations among these three aspects of religion.

The next two propositions are drawn from an article written by McCready and his wife and are based on evidence that not only the religious behavior of parents and especially the father, but also the relationship between the parents affects the religious behavior of the child in his own adult life:

10.5 *The most important religious socialization experience in childhood is the child's perception of whether the world is benign or malign.*

10.6 *This perception is closely linked to the acquisition of sexual identity. If the child perceives that sexual identity is easily lost, he will be inclined to be pessimistic or fatalistic in his religious stories.*

The McCready position is that the acquisition of sexual identity is a potential grace experience in which otherness may be perceived, but need not necessarily be perceived, as benign and gracious. Not only do subsequent life experiences of sexuality have the potentiality to be "sacramental," the acquisition of sexual identity can predispose a child to subsequent experiences of hope. If "otherness" itself has so arranged things that one can have one's "little boyhood" or "little girlhood" taken away easily, then the world is a nasty, unpleasant place, and otherness is not especially gracious. If, on the other hand, "little boyhood" or "little girlhood" is something to be rejoiced in and not defended tenaciously for fear that it will be lost, "otherness" is imagined as benign. My own story of being a little boy or a little girl is, in fact, a story of God.

The McCready perspective is intriguing both because it fits a good deal of data and is compatible with psychoanalysis. No further tests of it have been made, although there is some indirect support for it in the evidence that as sexual adjustment in marriage improves so does the shared religious imagery of the husband and wife grow "warmer."

The initial experience of sexual identity and the initial arrangement of religious symbols (quite possibly in the same process) are influenced both by the explicit teaching of parents and by the quality of the relationship between the parents and especially by the impact of the religious symbols on the life of the parents. The warmth and joy of family life and family sexual intimacy as perceived by a child is not only in itself an experience of grace, but also a predisposition for subsequent experience.

10.7 *Certain kinds of unhealthy or, at least, narrow psychological dispositions can easily be related to religious behavior, particularly when the family experience of the person has been harsh.*

While little research has been done on this subject in recent years, there exists a body of literature relating religion to authoritarianism, racism, anti-Semitism, and other forms of prejudice and emotional disorder. There is also the enormous clinical experience of psychoanalysts dealing with people whose emotional illness has fixated on religion. Finally, there is at least some evidence that certain personalities unable to cope with intense experiences of grace go through transient psychotic interludes after such experiences (which is perhaps one of the reasons why there is a tendency for psychoanalysts working out of their clinical experience to equate ecstasy with schizophrenia).

Charles Glock and his associates have repeatedly demonstrated a link between certain kinds of religiousness and anti-Semitism. However, Gordon Allport and his associates have distinguished between "intrinsic" and "extrinsic" religiousness, the former being religion orienting the person toward the cosmic power in his fellow humans, and the latter religion used as a means for social or personal control. It is, Allport has shown, the "extrinsically" religious who are apt to be authoritarian. Similarly, McCready has demonstrated that while an easy, optimistic world view may correlate with authoritarianism and racism, the hopeful world view tends to exclude such phenomena. In the terms being used in this theoretical presentation, some religious stories open the personality toward greater sympathy for other human beings, while other religious stories close the personality in on itself. One would want to know the contents of the religious imagery in those who experience psychic disturbance or personality narrowness. Religious imagery is in substantial part a reflection of childhood experience. The early family is a sacrament. Warm families produce warm stories of God. Repressive families turn God into a harsh judge.

Are religious stories and a world view which articulates a response to life problems in terms of those stories merely a function of personality development? Are warm images of God the result of a well-integrated personality and cold images a result of a disturbed personality? Is the religion we have described thus far merely a function of the psychic health of an individual?

The McCready theory mentioned previously suggests a very close link between personal identity and cosmic perspective. Religious images that were separable from self-image and image of others would have relatively little power. There seems to be little point in engaging in the sort of psychological reductionism which would contend that religion is "nothing but" personality development, especially since religious images and world view may just as well influence personality development, particularly after the early years, as be influenced by it. While it is possible and desirable to sort out the flow of causality between religious imagery and self-imagery, particularly at times of life crises and potential personality reintegration or disintegration, all that such research is likely to prove is that self-image and cosmic image affect one another. For the purposes of the present theory it is sufficient to assert they are distinct, but closely interrelated.

10.8 *The basic symbol arrangement absorbed in the early years is tenacious. It might be modified by later experiences and by conscious effort (perhaps by psychotherapy), but the stories of childhood cannot be driven out of the preconscious completely.*

Our research on young Catholics shows that the religious imagination is strongly affected by the quality of the relationship between a child and his parents and between the parents themselves. Mary imagery, for example, is especially likely to be warm and intense if the mother was affectionate, devout, and had considerable influence on family decision making.

I know of no available evidence either of the tenacity of the childhood symbol arrangement or of the capacity to undergo modification in later life. We do have evidence, however, that happy marriages increase the propensity of young adults to have warm religious imagery. I hypothesize that even those who have formally disaffiliated from a religious tradition will still carry in their preconscious residual imagery from their childhood religious socialization. One can easily think of literary examples such as James Joyce, whose Irish Catholic imagination survived intact his apostasy (and who is alleged to have replied when asked why he did not try another religion, "I may have lost my faith, I have not lost my mind"). However, systematic evidence which supports this proposition does not presently exist.

10.9 *Religion is closely related to childhood experience (when stories of God are so profoundly affected by the story of one's own childhood). Revolt against parents frequently involves revolt against religion.*

John Kotre's *View from the Border* and NORC research on religious changes document the relationship between family unrest and religious disidentification. A church, Kotre points out, emits many different signals. Which signals a person chooses to focus on are a function of the experience he brings to the encounter with church. Kotre's disidentifiers and identifiers did not differ significantly in religious and moral values or in political and social attitudes, but they had different childhood relationships with their parents. In a revolt against parents, God easily becomes a surrogate father and the church a surrogate mother. One punishes the mother and father by endeavoring to punish God and the church. The preconscious creates a story in which alienation from the family and alienation from the church are part of one's quest for freedom and maturity. The more unrest that there was in the life of the family of origin, the more likely is religious revolt.

In childhoods in which there is little conflict, the stories of personal maturation do not seem to require that one break free either from God or church or family in order to achieve personal maturity. On the other hand, if one's stories of God are blended with stories of conflict, then it will be more likely that maturity will involve not only familial revolt, but religious revolt. Evidence to support this assertion is overwhelming in the various NORC religious reports, though the precise dynamics of the relationship between the two sets of stories is only dimly understood. Much of the anger that religious rebels feel against God and church is, in fact, directed at their mother and father.

10.10 *The more religious joy there was in the life of the family of origin, the more likely the person is to have intense experiences of goodness.*

Experiences which renew hope predispose a person to further experiences of hope. If one's experiences in the family of origin have been benign, if the family experience offers grounds for hope, then intense religious experiences (of the sort described by William James) are more likely in adult life. The correlation between joyfulness in the family of origin and adult religious experiences is documented in NORC research on mysticism.

10.11 *The more religious joy there was in the family of origin, the more satisfactory is the marriage or adjustment in the family of procreation. Warm religious images intervene between these two family experiences.*

This proposition was originally generated on theoretical grounds: A warm family of origin leads to warm religious imagery, which, in turn, leads to warm interpersonal relationships and marital intimacy. The prediction was sustained in NORC research on the young Catholic family. Loving parents are conducive to imagining God as a lover, and imagining God as a lover is both conducive to marital fulfillment and is reinforced by marital fulfillment. The size of the correlations are modest: Other factors are at work in producing both joyous images and joyous marriages. But the link between family of origin, warm religious imagery, and family of procreation is strong confirmation for the theoretical perspective presented in this volume.

10.12 *There is a tendency for the late teens and early twenties to be a period of religious disaffection linked with a larger disaffection to other institutions of the society. However, at the end of the twenties there is a tendency for many of the disaffected to return.*

This proposition was stated theoretically before the NORC study of young Catholics and confirmed for the Catholic population in that study. Religious devotion declined sharply for Catholics from eighteen to twenty-eight, as did affiliation with the Church and even warm religious images. However, between twenty-eight and thirty there was a sharp religious rebound normally accompanied by an increase in marital happiness and a resurgence in warm religious images. It was precisely among those happily married young Catholic families that religious devotion rebounded most sharply, and especially in those families where the husbands' and wives' religious imagery converged toward a joint family imagery of religious warmth. It was impossible to sort out completely the interplay of these three factors—experience of sexual fulfillment with the spouse, experience of a renewed warm relationship with God, and a return to religious devotion. However, they all were closely linked.

There is also evidence from NORC's General Social Survey of a tendency to return to religious devotion in the middle thirties. The return of the late twenties seems unrelated to the presence of children in the family, but the return in the late thirties seems partially influenced by the presence of children.

Data from a Gallup survey taken in early 1980 show that this religious "rebound" continues even into the late thirties, and affects Protestants as well as Catholics. However, the rebound is seen to be less sharp for Protestants than it is for Catholics.

10.13 *Therefore, just as the family of origin is the first primary institution of religious socialization, so the family of procreation is the second. The proposition about primary groups in the previous chapter is especially applicable not merely to the parent-child primary group, but also to the husband-wife primary group.*

McCready's research indicates that fathers influence children religiously more than mothers, but wives influence husbands more than vice-versa. Noting that mothers are the more effective socializers in matters of politics and drinking and fathers the more effective socializers in matters of religion, McCready has suggested that children look to the "non-specialist" for behavior cues. Everyone expects Mom to be more religious than Dad, and Dad to be more political and to drink more than Mom, so you discount a specialist and look to the non-specialist for appropriate behavior patterns. Perhaps, exactly the contrary speculation might be true of the wife-husband relationship. Since the wife is the socio-emotional specialist (at least to the typical American family), she is reputed to take the lead in establishing the religious ambiance of the relationship. There is also modest evidence that those with warm religious images are more likely to choose spouses who themselves are more devout, even before the family religious strategy emerges. We know virtually nothing about the "negotiations" and the dynamics involved in determining the religious posture of a family. One might expect, however, an outcome not unlike that of conversion on the occasion of a religiously mixed marriage: The more devout partner is likely to have the greater influence.

10.14 *The happier the relationship between the husband and wife, the stronger the religious influence on one or the other, the more likely is the influence to be positive in terms of religious devotion.*

It is not merely the case that in the happier marriage there is a tendency for "your" story and "my" story to become "our" story. The tendency is also for the joint story to be a warm and positive one, and for higher levels of religious devotion to be the result of that story. The family of procreation is the critical religious socializer in adulthood, and the warmer that family, the more positive the religious outcome. We now need three-generation data to determine whether warm religious stories have a tendency to be transmitted from parents to children to grandchildren through the mechanism of happy and hence "sacramental," "hope-renewing" family experience.

10.15 *It would appear that the direction of the flow of imaginative religious socialization in marriage is from husband to wife.*

In the first five years of marriage a husband with a "story of God" as a mother and lover is no more likely to have a wife with a similar story than a husband whose religious imagination does not contain such imagery. However, in the second five years of marriage there is a convergence between wife's and husband's stories, so that if the husband's stories of God are as a mother and lover, the wife's stories become much more likely to be the same, whereas if the husband's story is different, the number of wives who think of God as a mother and lover declines. In the first five years the percentage of wives who think of God as a mother and lover is around 20 percent, regardless of what the husband's story is. However, during the second five years of the marriage the proportion of wives who think of God as a mother and lover goes up to 35 percent if such is the husband's story, and down to 10 percent if such is not the husband's story.

Chapter Eleven
Sexual Differentiation

11.1 *Sexual differentiation is a prime trigger for experiences of goodness.*

Whether the oldest known sexual artifact is also a religious artifact is a matter of some debate. The grotesque female figurines found in France and Siberia may or may not be fertility symbols, and religious fertility symbols at that. But, surely in most of the primitive religions that are reasonably well known to us either from archeology or anthropology fertility is of paramount importance because the survival of the tribe depended on the fertility of the flocks, fertility of the fields, and fertility of the human members of the tribe. The primary importance of fertility made it inevitable that it would become a major religious symbol, a trigger of experiences of hope and a resonator which enables one to tell stories about that experience of hope. Otherness was often perceived as an aroused lover, both because the experience of otherness might be triggered by sexual experiences and because the otherness often seemed rather like an aroused lover. Not all stories of God have, of course, a sexual component, but many do, almost as though it is very difficult to keep sexual imagery out of our stories of God.

11.2 *Otherness is often experienced as simultaneously maternal and paternal, life giving and life organizing.*

Not all religions have masculine and feminine deities, but most do. Even Yahwism, which in its elite manifestation vigorously excluded all trace of sexual differentiation in its deity, in its more popular forms kept alive the memory of the "shekeniah" of Yahweh. In the scriptures the shekeniah was the "presence" or the "spirit" of Yahweh, but in popular, folk Yahwism the shekeniah was Yahweh's spouse and the "Holy Spirit" was imagined, more or less, as a consort of Yahweh. Even in the Christian tradition of the Holy Spirit this dimension of the deity is quasi-feminine, that of affection, tenderness, and love. Similarly, in Catholic Christianity the Virgin Mary's function often is to reflect the tenderness, the "socio-emotional" aspects of God. While only a minority of Roman Catholics (24 percent) imagine God as a mother (32 percent of the men and 24 percent of the women), the fact that at least not a trivial minority keep that imagination alive demonstrates that imagery of God as maternal and paternal, masculine and feminine, has remarkable durability.

The more likely one is to have had a religious experience, the higher one's score is likely to be on a scale measuring responses to the image of God as a mother and lover. However, the increase is much more dramatic for men than for women, so that in the absence of religious experiences women score higher on this scale than men. But, among those who have frequent religious experiences men score substantially higher than women. It may well be that a man with frequent religious experiences is constrained to think of God in womanly terms by the intensity of the demand which is perceived in such experiences, a demand which has been traditionally described by the great mystics as well as in McCready's interviews with contemporary mystics as erotic.

In the mythic cosmologies of the ancient religions, the world came into existence through the embrace—often a conflict-burdened embrace—between life-giving chaos and life-ordering cosmos. Just as a child is conceived between man and woman, so the world is conceived through the union, often violent, between masculine and feminine ultimate principals.

11.3 *There is, therefore, a tendency for otherness to be seen sometimes as male and sometimes as female, either as a single deity or as many deities, some masculine, some feminine, or as one deity combining maleness and femaleness and many other deities (saints, for example) who are either male or female.*

Men and women, then, imagine the deity as possessing qualities of the opposite sex as perceived in relationship with their own sex or of one's own sex also as perceived in relationship with the opposite sex. Men and women, thus, may well imagine the masculinity of God differently. They may also imagine the femininity of God differently. However, they tend to imagine God as relational (and did so long before the doctrine of the Holy Trinity), and see that relationship as both manifested in their own relationships, and as validating their own relationships. These assertions are richly documented in the religions considered by anthropology and the history of religions.

11.4 *In experiences of hope, The Other or "otherness" is frequently experienced with a passion and a demand that parallels human eroticism.*

As noted before, this eroticism may lead men who have had intense religious experiences to begin to think of God as womanly. A similar problem does not exist for women, since the cultural imagery of God available in the West enables them easily to think of God as manly and to articulate and resonate a "story" of God in which he seems to be making the demands of an erotic lover. On the basis of this proposition I would predict that if subtle enough questions can be found, future surveys will reveal much more erotic content in the ordinary person's "story of God."

11.5 *Just as human loves go through cycles and periodicities, so do apparently relations between humans and the "other."*

I have already noted the parallel and correlation between the cycle of decline in the research on the first decade of marriage and the religious imagination of the spouses. Perhaps, precisely because we know periodicities in all our human intimacies, we project such a model into our relationship with the "other."

11.6 *There is an empirical correlation between human love and divine love.*

If one defines operationally human as the experience of sexual fulfillment in marriage, and divine love as frequent prayer, these two are highly correlated, but only when the husband and wife share a passionate religious imagination.

11.7 *There are four dimensions in the experience of the sacred as woman — mother, bride, death, and virgin.*

This paradigm is a matter for a contemporary research agenda, rather than a hypothesis which can be considered proven. The paradigm itself has been used by Neumann in his book and adapted in my own book, *The Mary Myth.* The paradigm is an extremely useful model to subsume the various manifestations of the feminine deity in the anthropological and history of religions literature. There is no reason why it cannot be adapted for research on contemporary religious imagery.*

At a time when feminism is as culturally and politically important as it is now, it is both appropriate and necessary to reexamine the feminine deity and the feminine aspects of The Deity which abound in human religion. Feminine deities often seem more important (whether they are older or not is a matter that need not concern us in this book) because giving life is ultimately more primal and more important than ordering life. At the present time we report that a substantial portion (though minority) of young Catholic men and women think of God as mother.

---

* I will confess with some chagrin that in our study of young Catholic adults we did not make a vigorous attempt to pursue the analytic possibilities of this paradigm. I suppose that failure really proves that when a data collector turns theorist his data collection "story" and his theoretical "story" may well occupy different parts of his brain.

Chapter Twelve
Life Cycle

The creative imagination is fluid, dynamic, and endlessly changing. The images and pictures never remain the same, and the religious stories in the creative imagination change as one's life changes. Propositional and creedal religion remain immutable during adult life, but on *a priori* grounds we would expect religious stories to change as the person who tells the stories to himself changes. Thus,

12.1 *There are different experiences of goodness at different stages of the life cycle.*

12.2 *There are different sensitivities to the intrusion of goodness at different stages of the life cycle.*

12.3 *There are different responses to the ambiguity of goodness at different stages of the life cycle.*

12.4 *Different aspects of religious stories (symbols) and different linkages among the various stories seem to respond to the different needs of individuals at different stages of the life cycle.*

Little attention has been paid by social researchers studying religion to the life cycle phenomenon despite the importance of the life cycle paradigm in contemporary American life. The young seem less religious than the middle-aged in most reports and the middle-aged perhaps a little more religious than the old. Normally the lack of devotion among the young is attributed to a secularization process. With the exception of some work by Robert Wuthnow, no serious attention has been paid either to life cycle or to generational phenomena in religious belief and devotion. An approach such as the one presented in this book which stresses the religious imagination will necessarily be more sensitive to the life cycle phenomenon, if only because there can be little doubt about the change in the creative imagination as life experiences accumulate. They story of a person's life changes and, hence, the religious stories which give meaning to his/her life also change.

There does not seem to be any age correlation for religious experiences. The young, the middle-aged and the old are all equally likely to report the prayer increases as people grow older with the increase for women being sharper than the increase for men. Religious devotion declines during the early and middle twenties, then rebounds in the twenties. Warm religious images similarly decline, and then rebound. Furthermore, warm religious imagery also undergoes a decline in the middle years of the first decade of marriage, but rebounds vigorously, especially in those marriages where sexual fulfillment and marital satisfaction emerge from the crisis of the middle years of the first decade of marriage. Presumably there are other "mini-cycles" in the years after thirty. But these cycles remain to be investigated.

12.5 *On the basis of the scanty information available to us from the life cycle literature it would appear that after infancy the critical turning points occur in mid-adolescence, at the time of marriage, at the "turning thirty" period, and during the "middle years."*

Bernice Neugarten has recently written that it is a mistake to impose a single life cycle model on the American population, and that there are rather many life cycle models, some appropriate for some individuals and others for other individuals. It may well be that some completely escape the "turning thirty" crisis and that some face their crisis of the middle years, if they face it at all, earlier or later than others. If the approach suggested in this volume of the sociology of religion has any value, then research on changing religious imagery is critically important. We have already demonstrated that marital adjustment, sexual fulfillment, religious devotion, and religious imagery all interact one with another in complex, intricate, and as yet not fully understood ways. It would be of considerable utility to understand how religious imagery and life cycle phenomena interact at both earlier and later stages of life.

Chapter Thirteen
Conclusions

Since this book is a schematic presentation of a theory of the sociology of religion, little purpose can be served in a conclusion by trying to schematize even more succinctly the theory presented. However, it may be useful to distinguish between the purpose of my theorizing and that of some other sociologists of religion.

I am not concerned, as were some of the early theorists of religion, with explaining the historical origins of religion. Nor is my purpose to describe and account for a secularization which I do not think has occurred and for which I can find little in the way of empirical evidence. I have eschewed completely the evolutionary approach to religion which has preoccupied both of the two groups of theorists I have just mentioned. Doubtless, there have been changes in human religion through the course of time. Religion is not today what it was a hundred, a thousand, ten thousand years ago. I am sceptical that the change has been unidirectional, even more sceptical that it has been away from religious faith.

My approach to religion in this book has not been "supernatural." Unlike many contemporary theorists of the sociology of religion, I refuse to be committed at the beginning to a definition which would limit religion to the "supernatural," and limit the study of religion to a study of those kinds of attitudes and behaviors which pertain to "sacred." It seems to me that such theorists limit religion to a collection of attitudes and behaviors, many of them peculiar, in which some people engage for reasons which are frequently unaccountable, though probably having something to do with a fear of death.

Rather, I place myself in the camp of those theorists of religion such as Max Weber, Talcott Parsons, and Clifford Geertz as well as Peter Berger and Thomas Luckmann who see religion as meaning-seeking behavior, meaning which Geertz, at any rate, sees incoded in "unique" symbolic explanations. I go beyond Geertz (though he himself has gone beyond his first formulations in the same direction) in that I account for the power of these symbols by rooting them in experiences of grace which renew human hopefulness in a given individual biography. A person undoubtedly approaches such experiences, at least in his adult life, with a repertory of pictures and stories which he has inherited from his religious tradition, so that in adult life and perhaps even childhood (though not, perhaps, in early childhood) the propositions may chronologically precede experience and symbol. But the driving force of religion, I contend, is experiential, imaginative, symbolical, and narrational, not propositional; and, I submit, perhaps *the* fundamental testable proposition in my theory is that it is the religious imagination which will predict behavior, not religious propositions.

One of my students at the University of Arizona whose background and convictions were "atheist" protested this approach. Religion, he argued, had to be an explanation for the existence of the world, and he and other atheists rejected religion because they could think of other and more satisfactory explanations for the cosmos. I would admit to that student that propositional and philosophical religion is deeply concerned about explaining the existence of the world, and proving the existence (or non-existence) of God. However, I argue, such philosophical religion is derivative; religion in its psychological (and probably in its historical) origin is not intended to be an explanation of anything, but is, rather, a reaction to wonder, to mystery, to grace (all three of which are the different names for the same phenomenon—an experience which renews hope). Philosophical explanations may be valid or invalid, adequate or inadequate, true or untrue. They appeal primarily to the intellect. Awe, wonder, grace, death, and the apparent presence of otherness in such encounters appeal to, or more appropriately "seize," the total personality.

A religion of which one can dispose in philosophical discussions is a tame, intellectual religion. But, having thus resolved to one's satisfaction the philosophical debates, a person must still deal with the wonder or the grace which periodically endeavors to seize us. The sociologist cannot make any definitive comment about the metaphysical or theological nature of such grace. He can only report that it seems to continue to seize people in what often seems to be a passionately loving embrace at odd times and in strange places in the very midst of secular life, and that such encounters with grace do, indeed, have a significant impact on our secular life. Sociologists cannot explain in any ultimate sense such experiences. They must observe, however, that philosophical explanations have not eliminated them from the human condition, nor made them any less of a challenge about which all humans must decide.

Appendix

Selected Items from NORC Questionnaire

23. When you think about God, how likely are each of these images to come to your mind?

(CIRCLE ONE NUMBER FOR EACH WORD)

	Extremely likely	Somewhat likely	Not too likely	Not likely at all
Judge	1	2	3	4
Protector	1	2	3	4
Redeemer	1	2	3	4
Lover	1	2	3	4
Master	1	2	3	4
Mother	1	2	3	4
Creator	1	2	3	4
Father	1	2	3	4

24. Here are some words people sometimes associate with Jesus. How likely is each one of them to come to your mind when you think about Jesus?

(CIRCLE ONE NUMBER FOR EACH WORD)

	Extremely likely	Somewhat likely	Not too likely	Not likely at all
Gentle	1	2	3	4
Stern	1	2	3	4
Warm	1	2	3	4
Distant	1	2	3	4
Demanding	1	2	3	4
Patient	1	2	3	4
Irrelevant	1	2	3	4
Challenging	1	2	3	4
Comforting	1	2	3	4

25. Now think about Jesus' mother, Mary. How likely is each word to come to your mind when you think of Mary?

(CIRCLE ONE NUMBER FOR EACH WORD)

	Extremely likely	Somewhat likely	Not too likely	Not likely at all
Gentle	1	2	3	4
Stern	1	2	3	4
Warm	1	2	3	4
Distant	1	2	3	4
Demanding	1	2	3	4
Patient	1	2	3	4
Irrelevant	1	2	3	4
Challenging	1	2	3	4
Comforting	1	2	3	4

31. Here is a situation in which some people actually find themselves.
Imagine that this is happening to you. How close would each of the
following statements be to your own reaction to such a situation?

You have just visited your doctor and he has told you that you have
less than a year to live. He has said that your disease is incurable.

*PLEASE CIRCLE A NUMBER ON EACH LINE TO INDICATE IF THE
STATEMENT COMES* VERY CLOSE *TO YOUR FEELINGS,* NOT AT ALL
CLOSE *TO YOUR FEELINGS OR IS* SOMEWHERE IN BETWEEN *THESE
FEELINGS.*

	Very close . . . . *Not at all close*
A. It will all work out for the best somehow.	1 . . . 2 . . . 3 . . . 4 . . . 5
B. No one should question the goodness of God's decision about death.	1 . . . 2 . . . 3 . . . 4 . . . 5
C. There is nothing to do but wait for the end.	1 . . . 2 . . . 3 . . . 4 . . . 5
D. I am angry and depressed at the unfairness of it all.	1 . . . 2 . . . 3 . . . 4 . . . 5
E. I am thankful for the life that I have had.	1 . . . 2 . . . 3 . . . 4 . . . 5
F. I cannot explain why this has happened to me, but I still believe in God's love.	1 . . . 2 . . . 3 . . . 4 . . . 5

32. Here is another situation in which some people actually find themselves. Imagine that one of your parents is dying a slow and painful death. How close would each of the following statements be to your own reaction to such a situation?

PLEASE CIRCLE A NUMBER ON EACH LINE TO INDICATE IF THE STATEMENT COMES VERY CLOSE *TO YOUR FEELINGS,* NOT AT ALL CLOSE *TO YOUR FEELINGS OR IS* SOMEWHERE IN BETWEEN *THESE FEELINGS.*

	Very close . . . . *Not at all close*
A. They are in pain now, but they will be at peace soon.	1 . . . 2 . . . 3 . . . 4 . . . 5
B. Everything that happens is God's will and cannot be bad.	1 . . . 2 . . . 3 . . . 4 . . . 5
C. There is nothing to do but wait for the end.	1 . . . 2 . . . 3 . . . 4 . . . 5
D. This waiting is inhuman for them; I hope it will end soon.	1 . . . 2 . . . 3 . . . 4 . . . 5
E. We can at least be thankful for the good life we have had together.	1 . . . 2 . . . 3 . . . 4 . . . 5
F. This is tragic, but death is not the ultimate end for us.	1 . . . 2 . . . 3 . . . 4 . . . 5

33. Do you believe there is life after death?

(CIRCLE ONE)

Yes . . . . 1 — *ANSWER A*
No . . . . .2 — *GO TO 34*
Don't know . . . . .8 — *ANSWER A*

A. Of course, no one knows exactly what life after death would be like, but here are some ideas people have had.

How likely do you feel each possibility is?

168

(CIRCLE ONE NUMBER FOR EACH PHRASE)

	Very likely	Somewhat likely	Not too likely	Not likely at all
1. A life of peace and tranquility	1	2	3	4
2. A life of intense action	1	2	3	4
3. A life like the one here on earth only better	1	2	3	4
4. A life without many things which make our present life enjoyable	1	2	3	4
5. A pale shadowy form of life, hardly life at all	1	2	3	4
6. A spiritual life, involving our mind but not our body	1	2	3	4
7. A paradise of pleasure and delights	1	2	3	4
8. A place of loving intellectual communion	1	2	3	4
9. Union with God	1	2	3	4
10. Reunion with loved ones	1	2	3	4

118. Taking all things into consideration, how satisfied are you with your marriage these days? Would you say you are very satisfied, moderately satisfied, or not satisfied at all?

(CIRCLE ONE)

Very satisfied 1
Moderately satisfied 2
Not satisfied at all......................3

126. How would you rate your marriage on the following aspects of your relationship?

(CIRCLE ONE NUMBER FOR EACH PHRASE)

	Excellent	Very Good	Good	Fair	Poor
A. Ability to talk about problems with my spouse	1	2	3	4	5
B. Emotional satisfaction	1	2	3	4	5
C. Confidence in the stability of our marriage	1	2	3	4	5
D. Agreement on financial issues	1	2	3	4	5
E. Opportunity to express love and affection	1	2	3	4	5
F. Sexual fulfillment	1	2	3	4	5
G. Agreement on basic values	1	2	3	4	5
H. Ability to express disagreement without threatening the relationship	1	2	3	4	5
I. Agreement on religious issues	1	2	3	4	5

ANSWER THE NEXT QUESTION ONLY IF YOU HAVE CHILDREN

J. Agreement on how to raise children	1	2	3	4	5

Notes

I have provided a comprehensive bibliography (pp. 177–183) which contains the important books alluded to in the text. For specific subject groupings, I provide the author's last name and the title of his book after the appropriate chapter section number (below). For the most part, these deal only with publications providing data to support the assertions made in the text.

Chapter 2

2.1 McCready with Greeley, *The Ultimate Values of the American Population.*

2.3 Greeley, *The Sociology of the Paranormal: A Reconnaissance;* James, *The Varieties of Religious Experience;* Hay, "Some Problems Associated with the Study of Religious Experience"; and Hay and Morissey, *Reports of Ecstatic, Paranormal or Religious Experience in Great Britain and the United States—A Comparison of Trends.*

2.7 The most important books of Mircea Eliade are *Patterns in Comparative Religion, Myth and Reality,* and *Myths, Dreams and Mysteries: The Encounter Between Contemporary Faiths and Archaic Realities.*

For a discussion of the influence of religious experience on the propensity to hope, see Greeley, *The Sociology of the Paranormal: A Reconnaissance* and Greeley, *The Religious Imagination.*

Chapter 3

3.4 See especially Long, *Alpha: The Myths of Creation;* Campbell, *Explorations in the Mythological Dimension, Masks of God,* and *Creation Myths.*

3.5 Some of the material on religion as story can be examined in such works as Crites, "The Narrative Quality of Experience"; Scholes and Kellogg, *The Nature of Narrative;* Kurt, *The Narrative Elements in Religious Meetings;* Kermode, *The Sense of an Ending;* and Tracy, *The Analogical Imagination,* Chapter 6.

The pertinent sections of Greeley, *The Young Catholic Family,* are Chapters 4 and 5. See also the first six chapters of Greeley, *The Religious Imagination.*

3.7 Discussions of the struggle between good and evil can be found in Ricoeur, *The Symbolism of Evil;* McCready and Greeley, *The Ultimate Values of the American Population;* Wuthnow, *Experimentation in American Religion* and *The Conscious Reformation;* Tiryakian, *On the Margin of the Visible.*

Chapter 4

Descriptions of the experience of otherness can be found in James, *The Varieties of Religious Experience;* and McCready, *Modern Mystics.*

4.4 The correlation between religious experience and religious imagery is discussed in Greeley, *The Sociology of the Paranormal* and Greeley, *The Religious Imagination.*

4.6 For discussion of the nature of sacred time and sacred space, see Eliade, *The Sacred and the Profane* and *The Forbidden Forest.* The propensity of various triggers of hope is also discussed in Greeley, *The Sociology of the Paranormal.*

Chapter 5

5.1 The impact of the Mary imagery on behavior is described in Greeley, *The Religious Imagination.* Discussion of religious stories and heritages can be found in Shea, *Stories of God* and *Stories of Faith;* and Tracy's *Blessed Rage for Order* and *The Analogical Imagination.*

5.2 The importance of childhood religious socialization has been
5.3 demonstrated by McCready in *Faith of Our Fathers:* McCready and McCready, "The Origins of Religious Persistence." See also the materials on family in Greeley, *The Religious Imagination.*

5.4 Empirical confirmation of the propositions about the relation-
5.5 ship between the experience of goodness and religious im-
5.6 agery can be found in Chapters 4 and 5 of Greeley, *The Young Catholic Family* and throughout Greeley's *The Religious Imagination,* particularly in Chapter 3.

5.8 On the subject of religious organizations see Greeley, *The Denominational Society;* Zaretsky and Leone, *Religious Movements in Contemporary America;* Worsely, *The Trumpet Shall Sound;* and Hobsbawm, *Primitive Rebels.*

Chapter 6

6.1 Geertz, "Religion as a Culture System"; McCready, *The Ultimate Values of the American Population.* These are both pertinent to a consideration of the human propensity to form world views.

6.2 McCready's *The Ultimate Values of the American Population* demonstrates that world views do not necessarily correlate with denominational affiliation.

6.3 Correlations between religious imagery and both world view
6.4 and social attitudes are demonstrated in Greeley, *The Young Catholic Family,* Chapters 6 and 7, and in Greeley, *The Religious Imagination,* Chapter 10.

6.5 The propositions summarize a considerable literature on the
6.11 early history of Christianity, including, for example, books by James Robinson, Norman Perin, and Reginald Fuller.

Chapter 7

7.1 These propositions evolved at much greater length in Morgan
7.2 and Greeley, *Structures of Prayer.*

7.3 This proposition is confirmed in Chapter 3 of Greeley's *The Religious Imagination.*

7.5 The evidence for these two propositions is also to be found in
7.6 Greeley, *The Religious Imagination.* For a discussion of ritual as a source of religious experience, see Durkheim, *The Elementary Forms of the Religious Life* and Eliade, *The Myth of Eternal Return.*

7.8 Roger Chaillois' work is especially pertinent to the question of prayer and playfulness. So, too, is the work of Huizinga.

7.10 This proposition is documented in Morgan and Greeley, *Structures of Prayer* and in Greeley, *The Religious Imagination.*

Chapter 8

8.1 These propositions are a development of the presentation of
8.2 Emile Durkheim in *The Elementary Forms of the Religious*
8.3 *Life.* However, the use that is made of Durkheim's perspective could scarcely have been anticipated by the master.

8.4 An elaboration of my own perspective on the dynamic of the growth of religious institutions may be found in Greeley, *The Denominational Society.*

8.7 These propositions are digests of perspectives offered by
8.8 Thomas Luckmann in *The Invisible Religion* and by Parsons in his essay, "Christianity and Modern Industrial Society."

8.9 The importance of the family in religious socialization is documented in McCready, *Faith of Our Fathers* and in Greeley, *The Religious Imagination.*

8.11 Evidence about the congruence of religious relationships can be found in Rossi and Greeley, *The Education of Catholic Americans;* McCready, Greeley, and McCourt, *Catholic Schools in a Declining Church;* Greeley, *The Young Catholic Family;* and Greeley, *Crisis in the Church.*

8.12 These propositions are documented in McCready, Greeley,
8.13 and McCourt, *Catholic Schools in a Declining Church.*

8.14 This proposition is documented in Fee, Greeley, McCready, and Sullivan, "Young Catholics of the United States and

Canada" (unpublished report for the Knights of Columbus, 1980) and in Greeley, *The Religious Imagination.*

Chapter 9

9.1 This proposition summarizes the material in the Luckmann and Parsons essays mentioned above (7.8).

9.2 These propositions summarize a vast discussion in the sociology of religion. See Durkheim, *The Elementary Forms of the Religious Life;* Bellah's "Civil Religion in America"; Malinowski, "Social and Individual Sources of Primitive Religion"; Merton, *Social Theory and Social Structure.* Parallel discussion, of course, involves an ongoing dialogue between the Marxists and the Weberians. See *The Protestant Ethic and the Spirit of Capitalism.*

9.5 See Warner's *The Living and the Dead.*

Chapter 10

10.1 These propositions are documented in McCready, *The Ultimate Values of the American Population;* Greeley, *The Religious Imagination;* McCready and McCready, "The Origins of Religious Persistence."

10.7 See Glock and Stark, *Religious Belief and Anti-Semitism* and Allport and Ross, "Personal Religious Orientation and Religious Prejudice."

10.9 The relevant literature about religious disidentification includes Caplovitz, *Religious Dropouts,* Kotre's *View from the Border,* Greeley, *Crisis in the Church,* and Wuthnow, "Recent Patterns of Secularization."

10.10 These propositions are documented in McCready, *Faith of Our Fathers* and Greeley, *The Sociology of the Paranormal.* Also see Greeley, *The Religious Imagination,* Chapters 4 and 6.

Chapter 11

11.1 This proposition is established in Greeley, *The Sociology of the Paranormal.*

11.2 This proposition is established in Greeley, *The Religious Imagination,* Chapters 4 and 6.

11.3 These propositions are supported by data to be found in

11.4 Greeley, *The Young Catholic Family,* especially Chapter 8;

11.5 and in Greeley, *The Religious Imagination.*

11.7 This proposition is a summary of a theory argued at much greater length in Greeley's *The Mary Myth.*

Chapter 12

12.1 These propositions are supported in varying ways in data presented in Greeley, *The Young Catholic Family;* Greeley, *The Religious Imagination, The Sociology of the Paranormal;* and McCready's *Faith of Our Fathers.*

Bibliography

Books marked with one asterisk are some of the more useful recent writing on the sociology of religion. Books marked with a dagger are books one might consult for theories of secularization. (Benton Johnson summarized these in a paper presented at the American Sociological Association meeting in Boston, August 1977.)

ALLPORT, GORDON, and MICHAEL ROSS. "Personal Religious Orientation and Prejudice," *Journal of Personality and Social Psychology* (April 1967):432–442.

BARBOUR, IAN. *Myths, Models, and Paradigms.* New York: Harper & Row, 1976.

BELLAH, ROBERT N. "Civil Religion in America," *Daedalus* 96 (Winter 1967):1–21.

BERGER, PETER. *Rumors of Angels.* Garden City, N.Y.: Doubleday, 1969.

BETTELHEIM, BRUNO. *The Uses of Enchantment: The Meanings and Importance of Fairy Tales.* New York: Alfred A. Knopf, 1976.

CAMPBELL, JOSEPH. *Creation Myths.* New York: Thames and Hudson, 1977.

———. *Explorations in the Mythological Dimension.* New York: Viking Press, 1969.

——— and DAVID MACLAGAN. *Masks of God.* New York: Viking Press, 1969.

CAPLOVITZ, DAVID. *Religious Dropouts.* Beverly Hills, Calif.: Sage, 1977.

CHESTERTON, G. K. "The Accident." In *Selected Essays of G. K. Chesterton.* London: Collins, 1936.

COHN, NORMAN. *The Pursuit of the Millennium.* New York: Oxford University Press, 1970

CRITES, STEVEN. "The Narrative Quality of Experience," *Journal of the American Association of Religion.* 1971:29–307.

CROSSAN, JOHN. *In Parables.* New York: Harper & Row, 1973.

DURKHEIM, EMILE. *Elementary Forms of Religious Life.* New York: Free Press, 1954.

*EDWARDS, DAVID L. *Religion and Change.* New York: Harper & Row, 1969.

ELIADE, MIRCEA. *The Forbidden Forest.* South Bend, Ind.: University of Notre Dame Press, 1978.

*———. *Myths, Dreams and Mysteries: The Encounter Between Contemporary Faiths and Archaic Realities.* New York: Harper & Row, 1967.

———. *The Myth of Eternal Return.* New York: Pantheon Books, 1954.

———. *Myth and Reality.* New York. Harper & Row, 1963.

*———. *Occultism, Witchcraft and Cultural Fashion.* Chicago: University of Chicago Press, 1976.

———. *Patterns in Comparative Religion.* New York: Sheed and Ward, 1958.

———. *Sacred and the Profane: The Nature of Religion.* New York: Harcourt Brace, Jovanovich, 1968.

FAWCETT, THOMAS. *Symbolic Language.* Minneapolis, Minn.: Augsberg Publishing House, 1971.

†FENN, RICHARD K. *Toward a Theory of Secularization.* Storrs, Conn.: Society for the Scientific Study of Religion, 1978.

FULLER, REGINALD H. *Foundations of New Testament Christology.* New York: Scribner, 1965.

*GEERTZ, CLIFFORD. *Islam Observed: Religious Development in Morocco and Indonesia.* Chicago: University of Chicago Press, 1971.

*———. "Religion as a Cultural System." In *Anthropological Ap-*

proaches to the Study of Religion, Michael Bonton (ed.), pp. 1–46. New York: Praeger, 1966.

†GLASNER, PETER. *The Sociology of Secularization: A Critique of a Concept*. London: Routledge and Kegan Paul, 1977.

GLOCK, CHARLES Y., and RODNEY STARK. *Christian Beliefs and Anti-Semitism*. New York: Harper & Row, 1966.

——. *Religion and Society in Tension*. Chicago: Rand & McNally, 1965.

GREELEY, ANDREW M. *Crisis in the Church*. Chicago: Thomas More Press, 1979.

——. *The Denominational Society*. Glenview, Ill.: Scott Foresman, 1972.

——. *The Mary Myth*. New York: Seabury Press, 1977.

——. *The Religious Imagination*. (forthcoming)

——. *The Sociology of the Paranormal: A Reconnaissance*. Beverly Hills, Calif.: Sage, 1975.

†——. *The Unsecular Man*. New York: Schocken Books, 1972.

——. *The Young Catholic Family*. Chicago: Thomas More Press, 1980.

—— and GREGORY BAUM (eds.). *The Persistence of Religion*. New York: Seabury Press, 1973.

HAPPOLD, F. C. *Mysticism: A Study and Anthology*. Middlesex, England: Penguin Books, 1964.

HAY, DAVID. "Some Problems Association with the Study of Religious Experience," mimeographed paper, School of Education, Nottingham University (England), 1976.

——, with ANN MORISSEY. *Reports of Ecstatic, Paranormal or Religious Experience in Great Britain and the United States—A Comparison of Trends*. Nottingham, England: University of Nottingham, School of Education, 1972.

HOBSBAWN, ERIC J. *Primitive Rebels*. New York: W. W. Norton, 1959.

JAMES, WILLIAM. *Varieties of Religious Experience*. New York: Macmillan, 1961.

*Kelly, Dean M. *Why Conservative Churches Are Growing*. New York: Harper & Row, 1977.

Kermode, Frank. *The Sense of an Ending: Studies of the Theory of Fiction*. New York: Oxford University Press, 1968.

*Kirk, Geoffrey Stephan. *Myth*. Cambridge, England: Cambridge University Press, 1970.

Kotre, John. *View from the Border: A Social Psychological Study of Current Catholicism*. Chicago: Aldine, 1971.

Kubie, Lawrence S. *Neurotic Distortion and the Creative Process*. New York: Ferrar, Straus, and Giroux, 1961.

Kübler-Ross, Elisabeth. *Questions and Answers on Death and Dying*. New York: Macmillan, 1974.

Kuhn, Thomas. *Structure of Scientific Revolution*. Chicago: University of Chicago Press, 1970.

Kurt, Wesley. *The Narrative Elements in Religious Meetings*. Philadelphia: Fortress Press, 1975.

*Levi-Strauss, Claude. *The Savage Mind*. Chicago: University of Chicago Press, 1969.

†Lidz, Victor M. "Secularization, Ethical Life and Religion in Modern Societies," *Sociological Enquirey* 49:191–217.

*Long, Charles H. *Alpha: The Myths of Creation*. New York: Macmillan, 1969.

*Luckmann, Thomas. *The Invisible Religion*. New York: Macmillan, 1967.

Malinowski, Bronislaw. "Social and Individual Sources of Primitive Religion." In *Religion, Society, and the Individual*, J. M. Yinger (ed.), pp. 380–385. New York: Macmillan, 1965

Maritain, Jacques. *Creative Intuition in Art and Poetry*. New York: New American Library, 1955.

†Martin, David. *The Religious and the Secular: Studies in Secularization*. New York: Schocken Books, 1969.

Maslow, Abraham H. *Religions, Values, and Peak Experiences*. New York: Penguin Books, 1976.

McCready, William C., Andrew M. Greeley, and Kathleen McCourt. *Catholic Schools in a Declining Church*. Kansas City: Sheed & Ward, 1976.

———. *Faith of Our Fathers.* San Francisco: Jossey-Bass, 1980.

———. *Modern Mystics.* (forthcoming)

——— with ANDREW M. GREELEY. *The Ultimate Values of the American Population.* Beverly Hills, Calif.: Sage, 1976.

——— and NANCY MCCREADY, "The Origins of Religious Persistence: Sexual Identity and Religious Socialization," *Concilium: International Review of Theology* (Fall 1963).

MERTON, ROBERT K. *Social Theory and Social Structure.* New York: Macmillan, 1949.

*MOL, HANS J. *Identity and the Sacred.* New York: Free Press, 1976.

*NOTTINGHAM, ELIZABETH. *Religion: A Sociological View.* New York: Random House, 1971.

OTTO, RUDOLF. *Idea of the Holy.* New York: Oxford University Press, 1958

*PARSONS, ANN. *Belief, Magic and Anomie.* New York: Free Press, 1969.

PARSONS, TALCOTT. "Christianity and Modern Industrial Society." In *Religion, Culture and Society,* Louis Schneider (ed.), pp. 273–298. New York: Wiley, 1964.

*———. "Religion and the Problem of Meaning." In *Changing Perspectives in the Scientific Study of Religion,* Allan W. Eister (ed.). New York: Wiley, 1974.

PERRIN, NORMAN. *Rediscovering the Teaching of Jesus.* New York: Harper & Row, 1967.

PETERSON, PAUL E. *School Politics, Chicago Style.* Chicago: University of Chicago Press, 1976.

PHILIP, MORGAN S., and ANDREW M. GREELEY, *Structures of Prayer.* New York: Academic Press. (forthcoming)

POLANYI, MICHAEL. *Tacit Dimension.* Garden City, N.Y.: Doubleday, 1967.

RAMSEY, IAN T. *Religious Language.* New York: Macmillan, 1963.

RICOEUR, PAUL. *Freud and Philosophy: An Essay on Interpretation.* New Haven, Conn.: Yale University Press, 1971.

†ROBERTSON, ROLAND. "Religion in a Secular Society." In *Sociology of Religion*, Roland Robertson (ed.). Baltimore, Md.: Penguin Books, 1969.

†——. "Religious and Sociological Factors in the Analysis of Secularization." In *Changing Perspectives in the Scientific Study of Religion*, Allan W. Eister (ed.). New York: Wiley, 1974.

*——. *The Sociological Interpretation of Religion*. New York: Schocken Books, 1972.

ROSSI, PETER, and ANDREW M. GREELEY. *The Education of Catholic Americans*. Chicago: Aldine, 1966.

SAGAN, CARL. *The Dragons of Eden*. NewYork: Random House, 1977.

*SCHNEIDER, LOUIS (ed.). *The Sociological Approach to Religion*. New York: Wiley, 1971.

*——, and SANFORD M. DORNBUSCH. *Popular Religion: Inspirational Books in America*. Chicago: University of Chicago Press, 1974.

SCHOLES, R., and R. KELLOGG. *The Nature of Narrative*. New York: Oxford University Press, 1966.

SHEA, JOHN. *Stories of Faith*. Chicago: Thomas More Press, 1980.

——. *Stories of God: An Unauthorized Biography*. Chicago: Thomas More Press, 1978.

*SMITH, ELWYN A. (ed.). *Religion of the Republic: Is There an American Religion?* Philadelphia: Fortress Press, 1970.

STENSON, STEN H. *Sense and Nonsense in Religion*. Nashville, Tenn.: Abingdon Press, 1969.

*SWANSON, GUY. "The Experience of the Supernatural." In *Sociology of Religion*, Roland Robertson (ed.). Baltimore, Md.: Penguin Books, 1969.

TIGER, LIONEL. *Optimism the Biology of Hope*. New York: Simon and Schuster, 1979.

TIRYAKIAN, EDWARD. *On the Margin of the Visible: Sociology, the Esoteric and the Occult*. New York: Krieger, 1972.

TRACY, DAVID. *The Analogical Imagination*. (forthcoming)

——. *Blessed Rage for Order: The New Pluralism in Theology*. New York: Seabury Press, 1975.

WARNER, WILLIAM LLOYD. *The Living and the Dead.* New Haven, Conn.: Yale University Press, 1959.

WEBER, MAX. *The Protestant Ethic and the Spirit of Capitalism.* Translated by Talcott Parsons. New York: Scribner, 1930.

*WHITMONT, EDWARD. *The Symbolic Quest.* New York: Putnam, 1969.

†WILSON, BRYAN. "An Analysis of Sect Development." In *Religion and Society,* Louis Schneider (ed.), pp. 482–497. New York: Wiley, 1964.

WORSLEY, PETER. *The Trumpets Shall Sound: A Study of Cargo Cults in Melanesia.* New York: Schocken Books, 1968.

WUTHNOW, ROBERT. *The Consciousness Reformation.* Berkeley, Calif.: University of California Press, 1976.

———. *Experimentation in American Religion: The New Mysticisms and Their Implications for the Churches.* Berkeley, Calif.: University of California Press, 1978.

———. "Recent Patterns of Secularization: A Problem of Generations?" *American Sociological Review* 41(1976): 850-867.

ZARETSKY, IRVING, and MARK LEONE. *Religious Movements in Contemporary America.* Princeton, N. J.: Princeton University Press, 1974.

Index

Index

Index

Index

Serpent myth, 11, 12
Sexual differentiation, 28–29, 151–155
Sexual fulfillment, 59, 60, 86, 92, 147, 154, 158
Sexual identity, acquisition for, 84n., 141–142
Shared experiences, 119–121, 127
Shea, John, 3
Shekeniah, 152
Simmel Georg, 7
Sinai story, 85
Skepticism, 6
Social class, religious behavior and, 136–137
Social commitment, 99–100
Society, 131, 138
Sociology of the Paranormal (Greeley), 21
Stenson, Sten, 7, 43, 48
Stevens, Wallace, 57
Stoicism, 16, 63
Stories: see Religious stories
Structures of Prayer (Morgan and Greeley), 109
Sullivan, Teresa, 59
Swedes, 136
Symbols, 32, 45–47, 53–57, 74–76, 84–93

T

Terror of religious experiences, 48–49
Tiger, Lionel, 15–18, 49, 50, 67, 115, 116
Tillich, Paul, 77
Tracy, David, 7, 21–24, 57, 79
Transcendentalism, 72
Tribes, 124–125

Trumpet Shall Sound, The (Worsley), 49
"Turning thirty" crisis, 158, 159

U

Ultimate values, 63–66, 83
Unconscious, 37–41
Unsecular Man: The Persistence of Religion (Greeley), 10

V

Validity of religious stories, 4–6
Vatican Council, 89, 104, 129
Vernacular liturgy, 115, 116
Vertical community, 83–95, 107
View from the Border (Kotre), 145

W

Warm religious images, 59, 65, 89, 91, 98, 99, 109, 124, 136, 140, 142–144, 146–149, 158
Warner, Lloyd, 139
Weber, Max, 7, 134, 162
Women, role of, 65
Wonder, predisposition to, 26–27
Wonderful, 74–76, 78, 162, 163
Work ethics, 134–135
World view, 97–99, 143
Worsley, Peter, 49
Wuthnow, Robert, 158

Y

Yahwism, 152
Young Catholic Adult, The (Greeley), 74
Young Catholic Family, The (Greeley), 59, 74, 128

192